Y0-BOD-736

Bouncing Back

Wayne Rice

Mark Oestreicher

David C. Cook Church Ministries—Resources
A division of Cook Communications Ministries
Colorado Springs, CO/Paris, Ontario

Custom Curriculum
Bouncing Back

Unless otherwise noted, Scripture quotations are from the Holy Bible, New International Version (NIV), © 1973, 1978, 1984 by International Bible Society. Used by permission of Zondervan Bible Publishers.

David C. Cook Church Ministries—Resources
A division of Cook Communications Ministries
4050 Lee Vance View; Colorado Springs, CO 80918-7100
Cable address: DCCOOK
Series creator: John Duckworth
Series editor: Randy Southern
Editor: Randy Southern
Option writers: Stan Campbell, John Duckworth, Sue Reck, and Randy Southern
Designer: Bill Paetzold
Cover illustrator: Anna Veltfort
Inside illustrator: Joe Weissmann
Printed in U.S.A.

ISBN: 0-7814-5166-3

CONTENTS

Sessions by Mark Oestreicher
Options by Stan Campbell, John Duckworth, Sue Reck,
and Randy Southern

About the Authors

Mark Oestreicher is a junior high pastor in Pasadena, California, as well as a seminar leader and author.

Stan Campbell has been a youth worker for almost twenty years and has written several books on youth ministry including the BibleLog series (SonPower) and the Quick Studies series (David C. Cook). Among the books he's written in the Custom Curriculum series are *Hormone Helper, Just Look at You! What Would Jesus Do?* and *Your Bible's Alive!* Stan and his wife, Pam, are youth directors at Lisle Bible Church in Lisle, Illinois.

John Duckworth is a writer and illustrator in Carol Stream, Illinois. He has worked with teenagers in youth groups and Sunday school, written several books including *The School Zone* (SonPower) and *Face to Face with Jesus* (in the Custom Curriculum series), and created such youth resources as Hot Topics Youth Electives and Snap Sessions for David C. Cook.

Sue Reck is an editor for Chariot Family Products. She is also a free-lance curriculum writer. She has worked with young people in Sunday school classes, youth groups, and camp settings.

Randy Southern is a product developer of youth material at David C. Cook and the series editor of Custom Curriculum. He has also worked on such products as Quick Studies, Incredible Meeting Makers, Snap Sessions, First Aid for Youth Groups, Junior Highs Only, and Pathfinder Electives.

You've Made the Right Choice!

Thanks for choosing **Custom Curriculum!** We think your choice says at least three things about you:

(1) You know your group pretty well, and want your program to fit that group like a glove;

(2) You like having options instead of being boxed in by some far-off curriculum editor;

(3) You have a small mole on your left forearm, exactly two inches below the elbow.

OK, so we were wrong about the mole. But if you like having choices that help you tailor meetings to fit your kids, **Custom Curriculum** *is* the best place to be.

Going through Customs

In this (and every) **Custom Curriculum** volume, you'll find

• five great sessions you can use anytime, in any order.

• reproducible student handouts, at least one per session.

• a truckload of options for adapting the sessions to your group (more about that in a minute).

• a helpful get-you-ready article by a youth expert.

• clip art for making posters, fliers, and other kinds of publicity to get kids to your meetings.

Each **Custom Curriculum** session has three to six steps. No matter how many steps a session has, it's designed to achieve these goals:

• *Getting together.* Using an icebreaker activity, you'll help kids to be glad they came to the meeting.

• *Getting thirsty.* Why should kids care about your topic? Why should they care what the Bible has to say about it? You'll want to take a few minutes to earn their interest before you start pouring the "living water."

• *Getting the Word.* By exploring and discussing carefully selected passages, you'll find out what God has to say.

• *Getting the point.* Here's where you'll help kids make the leap from principles to nitty-gritty situations they are likely to face.

• *Getting personal.* What should each group member do as a result of this session? You'll help each person find a specific "next step" response that works for him or her.

Each session is written to last 45 to 60 minutes. But what if you have less time—or more? No problem! **Custom Curriculum** is all about . . . options!

What Are My Options?

Every **Custom Curriculum** session gives you fourteen kinds of options:

• *Extra Action*—for groups that learn better when they're physically moving (instead of just reading, writing, and discussing).

• *Combined Junior High/High School*—to use when you're mixing age levels, and an activity or case study would be too "young" or "old" for part of the group.

• *Small Group*—for adapting activities that would be tough with groups of fewer than eight kids.

• *Large Group*—to alter steps for groups of more than twenty kids.

• *Urban*—for fitting sessions to urban facilities and multiethnic (especially African-American) concerns.

• *Heard It All Before*—for fresh approaches that get past the defenses of kids who are jaded by years in church.

• *Little Bible Background*—to use when most of your kids are strangers to the Bible, or haven't made a Christian commitment.

• *Mostly Guys*—to focus on guys' interests and to substitute activities they might be more enthused about.

• *Mostly Girls*—to address girls' concerns and to substitute activities they might prefer.

• *Extra Fun*—for longer, more "rowdy" youth meetings where the emphasis is on fun.

• *Short Meeting Time*—tips for condensing the session to 30 minutes or so.

• *Fellowship & Worship*—for building deeper relationships or enabling kids to praise God together.

• *Media*—to spice up meetings with video, music, or other popular media.

• *Sixth Grade*—appearing only in junior high/middle school volumes, this option helps you change steps that sixth graders might find hard to understand or relate to.

• *Extra Challenge*—appearing only in high school volumes, this option lets you crank up the voltage for kids who are ready for more Scripture or more demanding personal application.

Each kind of option is offered at least twice in each session. So in this book, you get *almost 150* ways to tweak the meetings to fit your group!

Customizing a Session

All right, you may be thinking. *With all of these options flying around, how do I put a session together? I don't have a lot of time, you know.*

We know! That's why we've made **Custom Curriculum** as easy to follow as possible. Let's take a look at how you might prepare an actual meeting. You can do that in four easy steps:

(1) *Read the basic session plan.* Start by choosing one or more of the goals listed at the beginning of the session. You have three to pick from: a goal that emphasizes *knowledge,* one that stresses *understanding,* and one that emphasizes *action.* Choose one or more, depending on what *you* want to accomplish. Then read the basic plan to see what will work for you and what might not.

(2) *Choose your options.* You don't *have* to use any options at all; the

basic session plan would work well for many groups, and you may want to stick with it if you have absolutely no time to consider options. But if you want a more perfect fit, check out your choices.

As you read the basic session plan, you'll see small symbols in the margin. Each symbol stands for a different kind of option. When you see a symbol, it means that kind of option is offered for that step. Turn to the options section (which can be found immediately following the Repro Resources for each session), look for the category indicated by the symbol, and you'll see that option explained.

Let's say you have a small group, mostly guys who get bored if they don't keep moving. You'll want to keep an eye out for three kinds of options: Small Group, Mostly Guys, and Extra Action. As you read the basic session, you might spot symbols that tell you there are Small Group options for Step 1 and Step 3—maybe a different way to play a game so that you don't need big teams, and a way to cover several Bible passages when just a few kids are looking them up. Then you see symbols telling you that there are Mostly Guys options for Step 2 and Step 4—perhaps a substitute activity that doesn't require too much self-disclosure, and a case study guys will relate to. Finally you see symbols indicating Extra Action options for Step 2 and Step 3—maybe an active way to get kids' opinions instead of handing out a survey, and a way to act out some verses instead of just looking them up.

After reading the options, you might decide to use four of them. You base your choices on your personal tastes and the traits of your group that you think are most important right now. **Custom Curriculum** offers you more options than you'll need, so you can pick your current favorites and plug others into future meetings if you like.

(3) *Use the checklist.* Once you've picked your options, keep track of them with the simple checklist that appears at the end of each option section (just before the start of the next session plan). This little form gives you a place to write down the materials you'll need, too—since they depend on the options you've chosen.

(4) *Get your stuff together.* Gather your materials; photocopy any Repro Resources (reproducible student sheets) you've decided to use. And . . . you're ready!

The Custom Curriculum Challenge

Your kids are fortunate to have you as their leader. You see them not as a bunch of generic teenagers, but as real, live, unique kids. You care whether you really connect with them. That's why you're willing to take a few extra minutes to tailor your meetings to fit.

It's a challenge to work with real, live kids, isn't it? We think you deserve a standing ovation for taking that challenge. And we pray that **Custom Curriculum** helps you shape sessions that shape lives for Jesus Christ and His kingdom.

—The Editors

If at First You Don't Succeed . . .

by Wayne Rice

You hold in your hand a great curriculum for junior highers. What makes it great is not so much the quality of the writing, the creativity of the ideas, or even the way it's organized. What's great is the relevance of the topic. *Bouncing Back* is about failure or "messing up"—and that's something every junior higher can relate to. After all, junior highers mess up *a lot.*

In fact, failure is something of a defining characteristic of early adolescence. If a junior higher messes up, it's a good sign he or she is normal. Psychologists who study eleven to fourteen year olds usually describe early adolescence as a "transitional" stage of life. What they mean is junior highers are in the process of leaving behind their childhood and becoming adults. They do this primarily by the trial-and-error method, with emphasis on the "error" part. Junior highers are trying on all kinds of personalities, beliefs, and behaviors in order to establish an identity of their own and to find their new place in the world. It's not an easy task, and most kids find the road to adulthood to be a rough one—full of potholes, detours, and an occasional head-on collision.

Do you remember what it was like to be a junior higher? I sure do. I remember vividly the embarrassments and frustrations of trying to make friends, trying to be accepted by other kids, trying to look cool, trying to become independent of my parents, trying to deal with my emerging sexual feelings, trying to be a good Christian. I tried hard at all of these things, but usually did or said the wrong thing, hurt somebody, and only made things worse. Almost always I ended up feeling guilty, discouraged, and not a little bit foolish.

Then I would go to church or Sunday school and feel even worse. I would hear stories about people who always did the right thing and who lived the Successful Christian Life. Good Christians don't sin, I was led to believe, or at least they don't sin very much. If they did sin, they were extremely minor sins, more like little mistakes that were forgiven instantly or hardly worth forgiving at all. I wondered what was wrong with me. My sins were big sins, not little ones, and I just knew that I could never have a relationship with God like all of these other people. Maybe someday I could, when I became an adult, but not now. It was just too hard while you were still a kid. So I pretty much gave up on trying to live the Successful Christian Life.

You may have some kids in your junior high group who feel that way right now. They may be on the verge of throwing in the towel. According to researchers, dropping out of church peaks during the junior high years. You may also have kids who have been so devastated by their failures, or the failures of others, that they have become angry, depressed, or even suicidal.

If you have kids who are struggling with failure, *Bouncing Back* will provide some real encouragement for them. As you spend the next few weeks dealing with the topic of failure, you can help your group members understand some of the following concepts.

God Doesn't Expect Immediate Perfection out of You and neither Do I

Failure is OK. In fact, it is expected. The Bible says that we are all sinners (Romans 3:23), which is another way of saying that people mess up a lot more than they think they do. Some people (especially religious people) like to think that they never mess up, which is why God continues to remind us that we do. That's also why God sent His perfect Son to die for us and to save us from all of our failures. Thanks to Jesus, we don't have to pay the penalty for all the times we messed up. Instead, when we get to heaven, we will be perfect in the eyes of God even though we have all been a bunch of failures. That's what grace is all about.

You can demonstrate the grace of God in your group or class by the way you relate to your junior highers. Let them know that you like them even though they mess up frequently. Junior highers can't be expected to act like adults. They are junior highers. Over the years, I have had very few serious discipline problems with junior highers simply because I allowed them to be themselves. Sure, there were kids who talked when they weren't supposed to, who made disgusting noises in the middle of my meetings, who passed notes in class, who made insulting remarks to each other, and so on. But I rarely had discipline problems. I didn't punish kids for being kids. Instead, I tried to understand, to help them learn from their mistakes, and to affirm their behavior whenever it was positive. If you catch kids in the act of doing good rather than always catching them doing something bad, kids will be encouraged toward good behavior. I'm not saying you shouldn't have rules and shouldn't try to maintain order in the classroom or in the church. But rules need to be enforced with grace and understanding that reflects the love of God.

Failure Isn't Fatal

Failure doesn't have to have the last word. Failure can be your teacher rather than your executioner. Failures can become stepping-stones to success. You can learn from your failures.

In this regard, junior highers can be taught the meaning of commitment. Commitment has a lot more to do with failure than it does with success. If you are committed to something, then you hang in there and keep going even when things aren't going too well. Historians tell us that the inventor Thomas Edison made over nine hundred light bulbs that didn't work before he finally made one that actually did. In other words, he *failed* nine hundred times! Although he must have been discouraged at times, he stayed with it simply because he was committed to inventing a light bulb. He didn't give up.

The Christian life is a lot like that. You don't get it right the first time or even the second. Every time Edison made a light bulb that didn't work, he learned one more way *not* to make a light bulb. It was actually a positive experience. Failure became his teacher. Maybe what we need to do is to help our junior highers learn from their mistakes, rather than to be defeated by them. Our emphasis should be on commitment—hanging in there. Spiritual growth takes time.

In Ben Patterson's book *Waiting*, the story is told of a young man who was appointed to the presidency of a bank at the tender age of thirty-two. The promotion was far beyond his wildest dreams and very frightening to him, so he went to the venerable old chairman of the board to ask for advice on how to be a good bank president.

"What is the most important thing for me to do as a new president?" he asked the older man.

"Make right decisions" was the gentleman's terse answer.

The young man thought about that for a moment and said, "Thank you very much; that is very helpful. But can you be a bit more specific? How do I make right decisions?"

The wise old man answered, "Experience!"

Exasperated, the young president said, "But sir, that is why I'm here. I don't have the experience I need to make right decisions. How do I get experience?"

"Wrong decisions," came the old man's reply.

Junior highers need to know that spiritual growth and maturity doesn't come easily. It usually comes by making mistakes and failing over and over again. The key to success is not how many times you fail, but what happens *when* you fail. If you learn from your mistakes and keep going, you are living the Successful Christian Life.

If You Fail a Lot, You're in Good Company

At the funeral of one great man in American history, the eulogy included these words: *"Here lies the most perfect ruler of men the world has ever seen."* Of whom was this said?

When he was 22, he lost his job as a store clerk. He applied for law school, but was turned down because his education wasn't good enough.

At 23, he went into debt to become a partner in a small store which failed. Three years later, his partner died, leaving him with the debt that took him years to repay.

At 28, after falling in love with a young lady and courting her for four years, he asked her to marry him. She said no.

He embarked upon a political career, and at age 37, on his third try, he was finally elected to Congress. Two years later, he ran again and was defeated. He suffered a nervous breakdown.

At 41, he ran for the position of county land officer and lost.

At age 45, he ran for the Senate and lost.

Two years later, he sought the nomination for Vice President of the United States and was defeated.

At 49, he ran for the Senate again—and lost again.

But at age 51, against all odds, he was elected President of the United States. He never finished his second term, however, because he was assassinated.

By now, you know who I'm describing—the most inspirational and highly regarded president in American history, Abraham Lincoln.

It is probable that if you took the names of history's most respected people—those whom we all regard as heroes—you would have some names that belong in the Failure Hall of Fame. What made Abraham Lincoln great is that he did not allow failure to destroy him.

Scripture is rich with examples of people like this, who failed miserably yet achieved great things for God. Abraham, the founder of Israel who was called "the friend of God," was once a worshiper of idols. Joseph had an ego problem, ended up in prison, and became prime minister of Egypt. Moses was a murderer, but later was the one whom God used to free the Israelites from slavery. Jephthah was an illegitimate child who joined a gang of thugs before God chose him to be his representative. Rahab was a prostitute who was later used in such a mighty way that God listed her in His hall of fame in Hebrews 11. Jonah and John Mark were missionaries who quit—but God used them anyway. Peter denied Christ three times and cursed Him, only to become a great spokesman for the early church. Paul was such a scoundrel that it took a long time before the other disciples would believe that he was truly a Christian. The files of heaven are filled with stories of great people who were once great failures.

As you spend the next few weeks with your group members in *Bouncing Back*, share some of your own story with them. Let your junior highers know that you are no stranger to failure. Let them know that if they fail a lot, they are on the right track. It only means they are alive. Failure is usually a prerequisite for greatness. There are some people who might say that Jesus Christ failed because He was executed by the Romans after only three short years of ministry. But we know better, don't we?

Let your junior highers know that they can look forward to a time when their failures will become victories, or as Robert Schuller has put it, their "scars will be turned into stars." That's the good news of the Gospel. Junior highers need to know that failure is normal, and that when they do mess up, they can rest assured that God loves them still. They need to know that when they make mistakes, they can learn from them. And they need to know that when they sin, they can receive forgiveness and a fresh start. No matter how great their failures, they need to know that God is greater yet.

Wayne Rice is cofounder of Youth Specialties and author of several books including Junior High Ministry *and* Enjoy Your Middle Schooler. *He also conducts seminars for parents called "Understanding Your Teenager."*

The images on these two pages are designed to help you promote this course within your church and community. Feel free to photocopy anything here and adapt it to fit your publicity needs. The stuff on this page could be used as a flier that you send or hand out to kids—or as a bulletin insert. The stuff on the next page could be used to add visual interest to newsletters, calendars, bulletin boards, or other promotions. Be creative and have fun!

Ever Had One of Those Days?

Does the thought of embarrassing yourself in front of others send shivers up your spine? Have you ever wondered how you could *ever* recover from a certain mistake or failure? Join the club! And join us for a new series called *Bouncing Back.* You may be surprised at what you learn about success, failure, and embarrassment.

Who:

When:

Where:

Questions? Call:

Bouncing Back

Bouncing Back

Ever feel like a failure?

Pass it on.

You've come to the right place!

It'll knock you out!

How Embarrassing!

YOUR GOALS FOR THIS SESSION:

Choose one or more

☐ To help kids recognize that everyone faces embarrassing situations.

☐ To help kids understand how to react when they're embarrassed.

☐ To help kids learn from the examples of biblical characters on how to handle embarrassment.

☐ Other _____

Your Bible Base:

Numbers 22:21-33
Matthew 14:1-12
John 3:1-3

How Much Would You Pay?

(Needed: Cut-apart copies of Repro Resource 1, chalkboard and chalk or newsprint and marker)

Have kids form small groups. Instruct the members of each group to share a really embarrassing situation that happened to them or someone they know.

After a few minutes, ask the members of each group to decide which of the situations they've shared is the most embarrassing. Then instruct them to put together a short skit acting out that situation. Give the groups about four minutes to prepare the skits; then have each one perform its embarrassing situation for everyone else.

After each group has performed, come up with a title for that situation and write it on the board. Leave space on the right side of the board for a column that you'll use later.

After all of the groups have finished their presentations, use your best judgment to give each group a rating based on how embarrassing its situation was (especially in comparison to the other situations). This rating should be in the form of a "price tag"—the more embarrassing the situation, the higher the price tag. Prices should vary from $10 to about $70. Make sure the combined amounts of the groups' price tags total much more than $100.

Then hand out $98 of "Embarrassment Bucks" (Repro Resource 1) to each group member. Say: **Let's pretend that every one of the situations that were acted out is going to happen to you in the next twenty-four hours. You need to decide which ones you would most want to avoid by paying the "embarrassment price." You don't have enough money to avoid them all, so you'll need to choose which are the most important for you to avoid.**

Give group members a few minutes to figure out which situations they'd pay to avoid and which ones they'd end up accepting. Have several group members share their plans and their reasoning. Let your kids keep their "embarrassment bucks" as a fun reminder of this session.

STEP 2

Embarrass-moments

(Needed: Copies of Repro Resource 2, pencils)

Hand out copies of "Embarrass-moments" (Repro Resource 2) and pencils. Read each situation aloud to your group members. Then give them a minute to write what they'd do in that situation. Ask several volunteers to share and explain their responses before you move on to the next situation.

After you've gone through all three situations, say: **Embarrassing situations are part of life—they're unavoidable.** This would be a great place to share an embarrassing story of your own to show your group members that embarrassing situations happen to everyone.

After sharing your story, say: **The problem a lot of people have—especially junior highers—is that the way they react in the midst of an embarrassing moment often makes the situation worse. Let's look at some people in the Bible who didn't handle embarrassment well. Maybe we can learn from their mistakes.**

OPTIONS

LARGE GROUP

MOSTLY GIRLS

EXTRA FUN

URBAN

JR. HIGH HIGH SCHOOL COMBINED

SIXTH GRADE

STEP 3

Embarrassment in the Bible

(Needed: Bibles, chalkboard and chalk or newsprint and marker)

Have group members turn to John 3:1-3 and read the story of Nicodemus coming to talk to Jesus.

Then ask: **What group was Nicodemus a part of?** (The Jewish ruling council.)

What did most of the Jewish leaders think of Jesus? (They didn't like Him; they were afraid of Him.)

Does it sound like Nicodemus believed that Jesus really came from God? (Yes.) **Why do you think Nicodemus chose to come to Jesus at night?** (Perhaps so that no one would see him.)

Explain: **Nicodemus had a fear of embarrassment. Apparently, he thought that if his ruling council buddies saw him talking to Jesus, they'd give him a hard time and make fun of him.**

Write the following on the board: "Fear of embarrassment might mean we care too much about what other people think of us." Then say: **Obviously, you can't live your life completely free from caring what other people think of you. But if you let other people's potential opinions control you, then you might make bad choices.**

Have group members read Matthew 14:1-12. This is a great story, but many of your kids probably won't know the background to understand what's going on. So after you read the passage, retell the story, filling in some information.

Herod was the king. John the Baptist was a prophet who talked about Jesus' coming and baptized Jesus at the beginning of Jesus' ministry. Herod had taken his brother's wife, and John the Baptist had the guts to speak publicly against Herod for doing this. Herod wanted to kill John, but was afraid of how the people would react. At Herod's birthday party, his new stepdaughter (Herodias's daughter) danced for the guests. Herod, in a flashy move to impress his guests, told her that he'd give her anything she wanted. Her mom had already coached her in what she should say if the situation arose—she asked for John's head on a platter. Herod knew he'd be embarrassed in front of his guests if he didn't follow through on his offer to the girl, so he had John beheaded.

Write the following on the board: "Fear of embarrassment causes bad decisions." Then ask: **Can you think of an example in your world of a time when a junior higher might make a bad decision out of fear of embarrassment?** (Drinking beer because kids might laugh at you if you don't; lying to avoid embarrassment; getting in a fight just so people won't think you're a wimp.)

Have kids read Numbers 22:21-33. Then ask: **How would you react if your donkey suddenly talked to you?** This question doesn't really have anything to do with the point of this session, but you have to address the obvious oddity in this story!

Who was with Balaam? (His two servants.)

How were the servants traveling? (On foot, alongside Balaam.)

Why did the donkey move off the path three times? (To save Balaam's life.)

Why do you think Balaam beat his donkey three times? (Some might suggest it was to discipline the donkey, but a beating wouldn't be necessary for this. Balaam was probably embarrassed in front of his servants because it looked like he didn't know how to control his donkey.)

Write the following on the board: "Our reactions to embarrassing situations might make the situation worse." Then ask: **Can you think of any examples in the junior high world in which this would be true?** (Yelling or hitting can make you look like a baby and cause you to lose friends. Trying to blame someone else can make you look like someone who won't take responsibility for his or her actions.)

What's the best way to react when you get embarrassed? (Some possibilities might include ignoring the situation or laughing at yourself.)

Advice Column

(Needed: Copies of Repro Resource 3, pencils)

Say: **Let's practice a little how best to react in embarrassing situations by giving advice to the three Bible characters we just looked at: Nicodemus, Herod, and Balaam.**

Hand out copies of "Dear Advice-meister" (Repro Resource 3). Your kids should still have pencils from Step 2. Have group members work in pairs to write advice-column answers to each letter. After a few minutes, have several volunteers share their responses.

Close the session in prayer, asking God for courage and strength for your group members to react well to embarrassing situations.

EMBARRASSMENT BUCK$

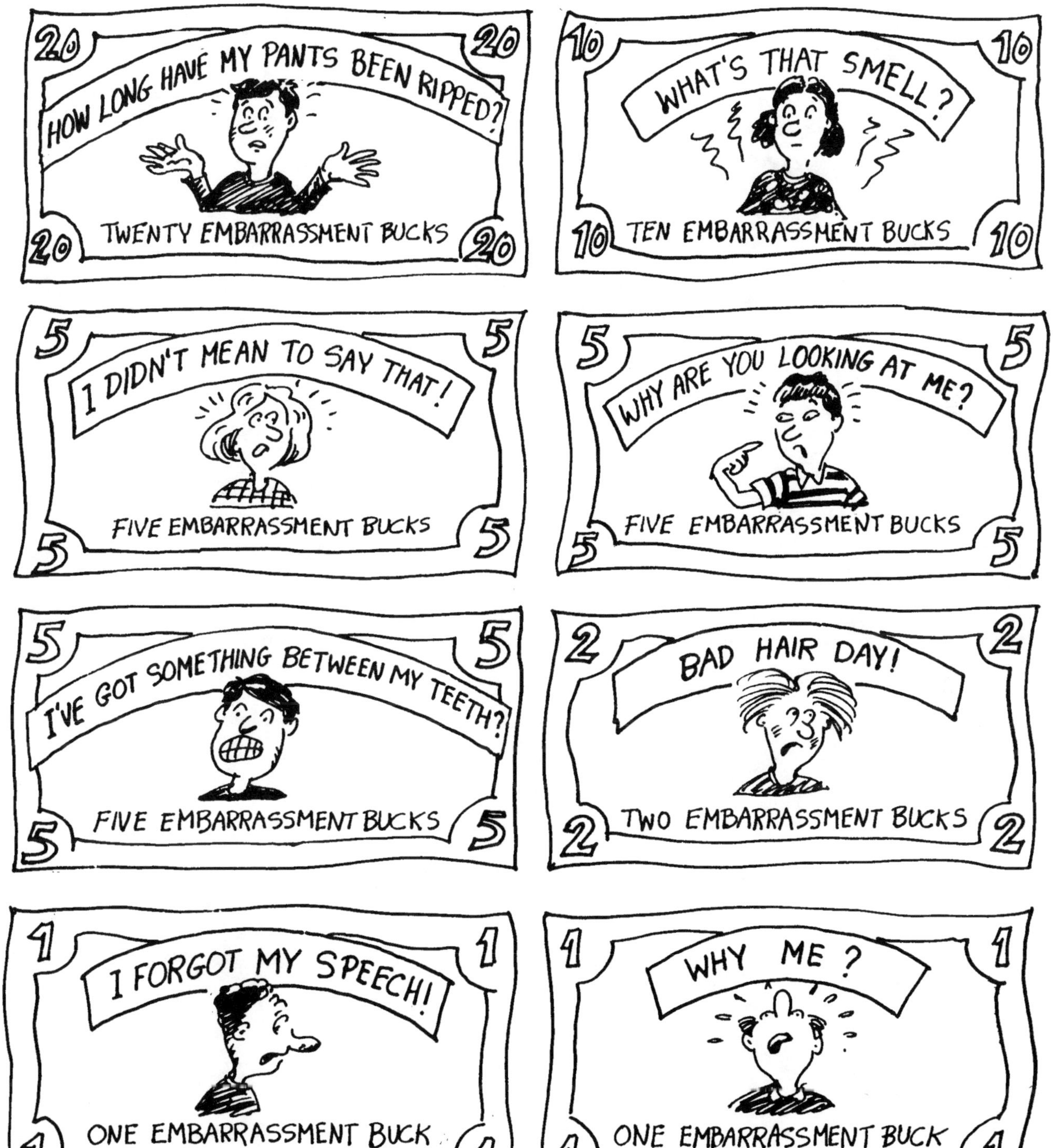

20 20
HOW LONG HAVE MY PANTS BEEN RIPPED?
TWENTY EMBARRASSMENT BUCKS
20 20
10 10
WHAT'S THAT SMELL?
TEN EMBARRASSMENT BUCKS
10 10
5 5
I DIDN'T MEAN TO SAY THAT!
FIVE EMBARRASSMENT BUCKS
5 5
5 5
WHY ARE YOU LOOKING AT ME?
FIVE EMBARRASSMENT BUCKS
5 5
5 5
I'VE GOT SOMETHING BETWEEN MY TEETH?
FIVE EMBARRASSMENT BUCKS
5 5
2 2
BAD HAIR DAY!
TWO EMBARRASSMENT BUCKS
2 2
1 1
I FORGOT MY SPEECH!
ONE EMBARRASSMENT BUCK
1 1
1 1
WHY ME?
ONE EMBARRASSMENT BUCK
1 1

EMBARRASS-MOMENTS

Embarrass-moment 1

You're a little sleepy today in school due to staying up late last night preparing two presentations for different classes. When your teacher calls on you to come give your presentation, she wakes you up from a momentary cat nap. You stumble to the front of the room and start rambling through a science topic you weren't very excited about in the first place: "The reproductive systems of whales." The teacher stops you after a minute and asks what your topic has to do with the Civil War. Everyone starts laughing as you realize you're making your science presentation in history class. What would you do?

Embarrass-moment 2

You're at a party with some popular kids you don't know very well, but would like to. Being a little nervous, you eat a few more nachos with bean dip than your stomach is happy to receive. You make a break for the bathroom just in time. Coming out of the bathroom, you feel a whole lot better, but you realize the bathroom really stinks now. You close the door and hope no one goes in there for a while. But ten seconds later, the prettiest, most popular girl in school opens the door to the bathroom and shouts, "Oh, gross! I think something died in here! Who was in here?" Everyone stares at you. What would you do?

Embarrass-moment 3

You're really thirsty and beg your math teacher to let you go get a drink of water. He's been frustrated with kids using that as an excuse to leave class for long periods of time. He says you can go if you're back within two minutes; if you're not, you'll get a detention. You run to the drinking fountain, but something's wrong with it. When you push the button, it splashes you in the crotch of your pants, making it look like you "had an accident." You have less than one minute to get back to math class. What would you do?

Dear Advice-meister

Dear Advice-meister:
My name is Nicodemus, but I prefer to be called Nick. This Jesus —I'm pretty sure He really comes from God. Unfortunately, all of my pals think He's a wacko. I know they'd never let me hear the end of it if they knew I went to see Him. What should I do?

Sincerely,
Nick-at-Nite

Dear Advice-meister:
My name is Balaam. (Don't rub it in—I know it's a dorky name.) My problem sounds dumb—it's my donkey. She keeps wandering off the road and making me look like I don't know what I'm doing right in front of my servants. What should I do?

Sincerely,
Donkey Problems

Dear Advice-meister:
I'm sure you know me—I'm Herod, the King. Here's my problem: I'm sitting at my own birthday bash, having a great time. My cute little step-daughter comes in and does this beautiful dance for me and my guests. My guests totally love her, so I'm thinking, Here's my chance to impress them. I offer her anything she wants! (Kinda stupid, huh?) I thought she'd ask for her own telephone line or for a few CDs. But no, she asks for the head of this prophet named John. I'm afraid to kill the guy, but I know my guests will think I'm a total wimp if I back down on my promise. What do I do?

Sincerely,
Herod

Step 1

Bring in a "Stretch Armstrong" doll (available where toys are sold). The arms and legs of this figure are designed to be stretched to great lengths; they then return to their original shape. Have kids form two teams. At your signal, each team should pull an arm as far as it can. At a second signal from you, teams should let the arms go. The winning team is the one whose arm "bounces back" more quickly. (In case of a tie, let teams try again with the legs.) Use this activity as a way to introduce the topic of "bouncing back" from embarrassment. If you can't find a Stretch Armstrong doll, bring in two or more basketballs in various stages of deflation. Have kids form teams for a basketball dribbling relay race. Teams with the most deflated basketballs will no doubt complain about their disadvantage; if you like, give everyone a prize after the contest. Use this activity to introduce the idea that our ability to "bounce back" from embarrassment is affected by the resources inside us.

Step 4

You'll need a large padded exercise mat and several banana peels for this activity. First, choose something that all of your kids know by heart (the Pledge of Allegiance, lyrics to a TV theme song, etc.). Explain that the object of this contest is to recite the words in the calmest voice possible, without pausing—while slipping on a banana peel, falling down, and getting up. Place a banana peel on the mat. Let your first contestant give it a try; then applaud him or her. Bring out a new banana peel, if necessary, and repeat the process with the next contestant. Award a prize to the person who shows the most grace under fire. Use this activity as a reminder that one good way to deal with our embarrassments is to ignore them and just keep going.

Step 1

To begin the session, have kids tell three stories instead of one. Two should be made up (or accounts of things that happened to other people). One should be a true story of an embarrassing thing that actually happened to the person. After each person tells three stories, the other group members should vote for the story they believe is true about the person. Keep score to see who has the most correct guesses. Make a note of all the stories, real and imagined, for the "price tag" activity that follows. With each person providing three stories instead of one, you should have plenty of embarrassing situations to choose from.

Step 4

Instead of having kids write out their advice, designate your group members to be a "panel of experts." Line up chairs as if your kids were appearing on "Oprah"; then read one situation at a time from Repro Resource 3. Let kids respond at will. Some kids may respond to every situation. But if you see that some people are not responding at all, you may need to ask specifically what advice they would recommend in one of the situations. Since group members don't have to write down everything they want to say, you should be able to cover more territory. If this is true, create some potentially embarrassing situations of your own and let your panel of experts offer advice about them after they discuss the biblical scenarios listed on Repro Resource 3.

Step 1

Rather than using the Repro Resource 1 activity, try a different approach. Have kids form small groups. Instruct each group to come up with the most embarrassing situation possible for a junior high kid. Encourage group members to be creative and humorous (but not offensive or disgusting) in their scenarios. After a few minutes, have each group share its scenario. If possible, ask a few adults from your church to serve as a panel of judges for this activity. If that's not possible, you should judge the activity yourself to determine which was the most embarrassing situation. Award prizes to the winning group. Afterward, ask volunteers to share some of the most embarrassing situations they or people they know have faced. Then move on to Step 2.

Step 2

Have kids form three groups. Assign each group one of the situations on Repro Resource 2. After reading its assigned situation, each group should come up with (a) the worst possible response or thing to do in that situation, and (b) the best possible response or thing to do in that situation. After a few minutes, have each group share what it came up with. Allow other group members to comment on the suggestions.

Step 3

Kids may think of Bible characters like Nicodemus, Herod, and Balaam as unreal, older people whose feelings of embarrassment couldn't possibly match their own. Help kids see the humanness of the Bible characters you study; to make it easier, you may want to choose one or more of the following to replace the characters in the session plan: (1) A young follower of Jesus fled at Jesus' arrest, losing his clothes in the process (Mark 14:51, 52). Some suggest that this was John Mark, writer of the Gospel of Mark, who later made another mistake—deserting Paul and Barnabas on a missionary trip (Acts 13:13). (2) Mary, the young mother of Jesus, had reason to be embarrassed when she became pregnant while unmarried (Luke 1:26-38). Yet she trusted God enough to sing a song glorifying Him (Luke 1:46-55). (3) Young David must have looked silly trying to wear Saul's armor (I Samuel 17:38, 39a), but instead of being embarrassed he took it off and kept going toward his goal (I Samuel 17:39b-50).

Step 4

Jaded kids may question the point of giving advice to three dead people who didn't even ask for it. Instead, discuss how kids could have reacted most constructively to the real-life embarrassing situations they shared in Step 1. Should they have cared less about what others thought? Could they have taken time out to plan their responses more carefully? What steps can they take to react more thoughtfully and less emotionally the next time they're embarrassed? What do they need to trust God for (friends, acceptance, confidence, etc.) in order to fear embarrassment less?

Step 3

Of the three Bible stories covered in this step, the session provides background material for one of them. But if your group members don't know a lot about Scripture, you'll probably want to be prepared to summarize the stories of Nicodemus and Balaam as well as the death of John the Baptist. You should be sure to point out that because Nicodemus risked embarrassment to go see Jesus, we have the most quoted verse of the Bible. Explain that John 3:16 is part of Jesus' response to the questions Nicodemus was asking Him during this secret visit. Also let kids know that Nicodemus eventually responded to Jesus' love and concern. He was one of the two who took care of Jesus' body after His crucifixion (John 19:38-42). Also be prepared for any questions concerning Balaam's story. (See Numbers 22.) If kids don't show enough interest to ask about this odd story, you should try to generate some curiosity on their parts. Be ready to provide kids with references for reading on their own during the coming week (if anyone is interested).

Step 4

Rather than repeating the stories just covered in Step 3, you might want to write "Dear Advice-meister" letters from *other* biblical characters who suffered embarrassment. For example, you could use similarly updated language to describe Peter's embarrassment at not staying on top of the water in his stroll with Jesus (Matthew 14:22-33), the disciples' inability to remove an evil spirit from a young boy (Mark 9:14-29), and Eutychus falling asleep during a sermon and plunging off a windowsill (Acts 20:7-12). As young people see that there are all sorts of good stories tucked away in the pages of Scripture, they may be more willing to begin to search for them on their own.

Step 1

Before the session, prepare several pairs of name tags. On one name tag in each pair, write an embarrassing situation that someone may face. On the other name tag in the pair, write a positive response that another person might give to that embarrassing situation. (For example, on one tag you might write "You just stopped at Taco Bell and now have major burrito breath"; on another tag you might write "I just got these new breath mints. Would you like one?") Make sure you have at least one name tag for everyone in your group. As kids arrive, give each one a name tag. Allow kids a few minutes to find the right partner. When everyone is paired up, ask: **How many of you have ever been in an embarrassing situation? How did the people around you respond to your embarrassing situation?** Get a couple of responses. **How would you have felt if someone had offered you a kind word during your embarrassing situation?** After you get a few responses, explain that we all face embarrassing situations. In this session, you're going to take a look at how to deal with them.

Step 4

Hand out paper and pencils. Ask your kids to write a letter to God, telling Him of something they're really embarrassed about. It could be something they've done or something about them or their family. Emphasize to your group members that no one else will read what they write. When everyone has finished his or her letter, encourage kids to spend some time in prayer, asking God for His help with—and if needed, His forgiveness for—the situation. Assure kids that nothing is too big or too small for God to care about.

Step 2

Change the situations on Repro Resource 2 as follows:

• *Embarrass-moment 2*—You're at a party with some popular kids you don't know very well, but would like to. You're eating some cheese pizza when the cutest guy in school comes over and starts talking to you. You chat for a while, then he moves on. Ready to faint, you head to the bathroom and discover a big string of cheese hanging from your chin. What would you do?

• *Embarrass-moment 3*—It's time for the end-of-the-year awards assembly. You're getting a few awards—perfect attendance, honor roll, a volleyball letter—so you know that you'll be making a few trips to the stage. On the first one, however, you trip and fall flat on your face. The entire auditorium rocks with laughter. What would you do?

Step 3

After you've written the three results of fear of embarrassment on the board, ask: **What can we do to handle these fears?** As a group, come up with some practical ideas for overcoming the fear of embarrassment—specifically as it relates to caring too much about what other people think, making bad decisions, and reacting in ways that make the situation worse.

Step 3

When you get to the Bible story about Herod and the daughter of Herodias, stop long enough to ask your guys: **What's the silliest or most embarrassing thing you've ever done because there was a good-looking girl involved?** If your guys aren't willing to share stories about themselves, they'll probably be quick to do so about each other. The stories are likely to be funny and embarrassing, but try to show kids from the story of John the Baptist that sometimes guys do extremely wrong things out of misplaced loyalties or the desire to impress others (usually females). While your guys aren't likely to put someone else to death, they might reject or embarrass others to the point where those people "wished they were dead." Challenge your guys from this point on to be true to themselves and their beliefs, rather than sacrificing self-esteem for a little temporary attention from a member of the opposite sex.

Step 4

Skip the exercise on Repro Resource 3. Instead, use the time to try to initiate a little male bonding among your guys. They've already shared some embarrassing moments from the past, and they've seen what the fear of embarrassment can do if they aren't careful. Challenge them to rise above "normal" junior high behavior and stand up for each other during embarrassing or uncomfortable situations that may arise in the future. Many guys seem to thrive on putting other people down just to seem a little higher themselves. If your group members can learn to overcome this tendency, they may be quite surprised to see what a difference it will make in their lives during junior high and high school.

Step 1

Rather than having kids form groups to act out embarrassing moments from the past, have each person write one down, being as specific as possible. Group members should not see what others are writing. Collect kids' stories as they finish; read one at a time. (Be sure to include a tale of your own!) As you read each one, let kids guess who wrote the story. At that time, also determine the "price tag" as instructed in the session.

Step 2

After kids complete Repro Resource 2, have them select a topic such as "Embarrassing Moments in Television Sitcoms," "Embarrassing Moments in History," or so forth. Instruct each person to write a scenario similar to the ones on Repro Resource 2, but from a real or fictional character that others should be able to identify from a few clues. Provide an obvious example to give kids an idea of what you're looking for. Here's one from "Embarrassing Moments in English Literature": **Boy, do I feel stupid. We had such a good plan, or so we thought. We were young and in love, but our parents couldn't get along so they didn't want us to see each other. We were going to run away. With a little help, I took a potion that made me appear to be dead so that everyone would leave me alone. I was going to come to and join my man. But he found me and thought I was really dead, so he killed himself. I came out of my coma-like state, and there he was with a knife through his heart. Boy, was I embarrassed! Who am I? What would you do in my place?** English students should identify Juliet. But anything goes when your kids write scenarios of their own. They can create embarrassing situations for Bart Simpson, Batman, Queen Elizabeth, or anyone else they choose.

MEDIA

Step 1

Show a few goofs from a "sports bloopers" videotape (like *Football Follies, Super-Duper Baseball Bloopers, Baseball's Funniest Bloopers,* or *Greatest Sports Follies;* check your video rental store for availability). Be sure to prescreen the segments you plan to show. After playing them for the group, ask: **How would you feel if you'd made those mistakes? What do you think happened to the mistake-makers? What embarrassing moments from your own life are you glad people can't watch on video? When you see that even sports stars make errors, does it make you feel better about your own goofs? Why or why not?**

Step 4

Play and discuss one or more contemporary Christian songs that encourage kids to bounce back from failure and embarrassment and to trust God with their futures. Possibilities include "Tomorrow" (Amy Grant), "The Sky's the Limit" (Leon Patillo), "Every Step of the Way" (Billy Sprague or Kathy Troccoli), "Following the King" (White Heart), "Believing for the Best in You" (Michael and Stormie Omartian), and "Right Where You Are" (Kenny Marks). After each song you play, ask: **If you listened to this song after making an embarrassing mistake, do you think it might help you feel better? Why or why not? What is the message of this song for someone who makes mistakes? What reasons does the song give for being hopeful about your future?**

SHORT MEETING TIME

Step 1

Replace Step 1 with a shorter opener. Send one group member (the seeker) out of the room. The rest of the group members will then try to "hide in plain sight"—to stay perfectly still and blend in with their surroundings so well that they seem to disappear. When everyone's found a place, let the seeker in. The last person to be noticed and tagged by the seeker wins. Ask: **Have you ever been so embarrassed that you wished you could disappear or sort of melt into the floor? If so, when?** To save more time, skip Step 1 entirely and start with Repro Resource 2 in Step 2.

Step 3

Instead of reading and discussing three Bible stories, study just the story of Moses, who resisted talking to Pharaoh for fear of making an embarrassing mistake (Exodus 3:10-14; 4:1-5, 10-16). Discuss God's reaction—reassurance, offers to help, a reminder of His power, anger at Moses' continuing resistance, giving Moses a helper to go with him, and more promises of step-by-step guidance. Ask: **How do you think God feels about our fear of embarrassment? Why? What help does He offer us?** In Step 4, skip Repro Resource 3. Instead, return to the situations on Repro Resource 2. Ask: **What's the worst that could happen as a result of this situation? How could God help a person survive that?**

URBAN

Step 2

Add the following situation to Repro Resource 2:
• *Embarrass-moment 4*—You're walking down the street with some friends when you notice someone with long beautiful hair and a shapely body walking in front of you. You start talking about how beautiful she is and how much you'd like to go out with her. However, when the person turns the corner, you discover that it's a man. Your friends start laughing at you and threatening to tell other kids at school about the kind of person you'd like to go out with. What would you do?

Step 3

Ask volunteers to share some examples of embarrassing situations that escalated and even got out of hand because a person didn't know how to respond to embarrassment. For example, perhaps a person who was embarrassed at school sought revenge against one of the people who laughed at him. Or perhaps someone chose to live a lie rather than owning up to an embarrassing situation. After a few volunteers have shared, move on to the Bible study to see how Bible characters responded to embarrassing situations.

Step 2

For your high schoolers, add the following scenarios to Repro Resource 2:

• *Embarrass-moment 4*—You've just gotten your driver's license and are driving to school for the first time. As you pull into the lot, you lean over for just a second to turn up the radio, and take the steering wheel with you. The car jumps the curb and you wipe out a stop sign. Everyone in the parking lot is watching. What would you do?

• *Embarrass-moment 5*—You're picking up your date—it's the first time you've gone out—and she's not quite ready. You play it cool and talk with her parents for a few minutes. Everything seems to be going well. Then you notice that your fly is unzipped. What would you do?

Step 3

Before you get into the Bible study to see how biblical characters dealt with embarrassing situations, ask a few of your high schoolers to share some embarrassing situations that they experienced in junior high and explain how they dealt with them. If they see now that they could have handled the situations differently, encourage them to explain why a different response would have been better.

Step 1

Don't ask your sixth graders to share or act out embarrassing situations. Instead, before the session, you should create a list of embarrassing situations that sixth graders might face. Your list might include things like finding out in the middle of the school day that your pants are ripped, forgetting your lines in the school play, being the only person in your class to flunk a test, getting so upset on the playground that you cry in front of your friends, and other similar incidents. Assign each embarrassing situation a "price tag," based on how embarrassing the situation is—the more embarrassing the situation, the higher the price. Hand out the "embarrassment bucks" from Repro Resource 1. Then continue Step 1 as written in the session.

Step 2

Add the following situation to Repro Resource 2:

• *Embarrass-moment 4*—You're hosting your very first slumber party at your house. Everything is going great until your little sister announces loudly that you still sleep with a stuffed animal. Some of your friends start snickering and ask you if it's true. It is. What would you do?

Date Used:

Approx.
Time

Step 1: How Much Would You Pay? _____
o Extra Action
o Small Group
o Large Group
o Fellowship & Worship
o Extra Fun
o Media
o Short Meeting Time
o Sixth Grade
Things needed:

Step 2: Embarrass-moments _____
o Large Group
o Mostly Girls
o Extra Fun
o Urban
o Combined Junior High/High School
o Sixth Grade
Things needed:

Step 3: Embarrassment in the Bible _____
o Heard It All Before
o Little Bible Background
o Mostly Girls
o Mostly Guys
o Short Meeting Time
o Urban
o Combined Junior High/High School
Things needed:

Step 4: Advice Column _____
o Extra Action
o Small Group
o Heard It All Before
o Little Bible Background
o Fellowship & Worship
o Mostly Guys
o Media
Things needed:

2 Try, Try Again?

YOUR GOALS FOR THIS SESSION:

Choose one or more

☐ To help kids recognize the difference between moral mistakes (sin) and other mistakes.

☐ To help kids learn four important questions to ask about mistakes.

☐ To help kids apply the four questions to a pretend situation and to a real situation.

☐ Other _____
_____

Your Bible Base:

Genesis 4:3-8
Luke 22:54-62

No Mistakes Allowed

(Needed: Prizes [optional])

Have kids form two teams. Explain that the teams will be competing in a game in which no mistakes are allowed. You will ask each team a question. If the team answers the question correctly, it gets a point. The team with the most points at the end of the game is the winner. Emphasize that the team's first answer is the only one you'll accept. Players may not change their minds after giving an answer. Also emphasize that the teams must listen very carefully because no questions will be repeated.

Use the following questions for the game (or come up with some of your own):

Question #1
Rabbit, duck, penguin, elephant, zebra, porpoise, groundhog, antelope, minnow, water bug, and dog. How many of the creatures I just named spend most of their time in or on water? (Five.)

Question #2
Carl had six sisters—Elvira, Judy, Pam, Tracy, Patricia, and Penelope—and six brothers—Tom, Kurt, Franklin, Anton, Paul, and Peter. He also had a dog and a cat. Name three of Carl's sisters.

Question #3
I had the weirdest dream last night. In it, four monkeys rode across the bright orange horizon on horses named Buck, Chip, Frank, and Felix, while a flock of buzzards hovered overhead. The sheriff, a parakeet named Tex, walked up to me and chirped, "Howdy, pardner!" What was the second horse's name? (Chip.)

Question #4
Bacon, bed, butter, BMW, belt, box, bell, bean, bubble, bike, and broom. Name all of the items I just mentioned that you can eat. (Bacon, butter, and bean.)

Question #5
The rock group Fuzzy Bike Seat opened their concert with their hit song "That's My Lemonade." But then they played a bunch of songs that no one had heard before: "The Cost of Crying," "Your Face Is Killing Me," "Riding Shamu," "The Paw That Broke the Camel's Snack," and "Barney's Night-

mare." **What was the third song of the concert?** ("Your Face Is Killing Me.")

Question #6
Circle, square, triangle, oval, pentagon, and semicircle. What's the total number of straight lines of these shapes? (Thirteen.)

Question #7
Freda's half sister Karen said that Philip's cousin Sam called Trent to tell him that Sonia said that Maria likes him. Who's Philip's cousin? (Sam.)

Question #8
Shirt, wig, socks, underwear, bracelet, tie, sandals, slacks, necklace, hat, belt, and dress. Name the four items on the list that start with the letter "S." (Shirts, socks, sandals, and slacks.)

Question #9
I just read the book *Pets That Kill*. It was very scary. The first chapter was called "The Mouse That Munched." It was gross. The second chapter was "Cats That Carve." It was terrifying. These were followed by "Chainsaw Chimps," "Parrots That Poison," "Turtles and Trash Bags," "Dynamite Doggies," and "Hungry Hamsters." What was the second chapter? ("Cats That Carve.")

Question #10
Ping-Pong, in-line skating, pinball, cross-country skiing, surfing, softball, bowling, hang gliding, skateboarding, running, and swimming. Name the activities that involve a ball. (Ping-Pong, pinball, softball, and bowling.)

Award a bag of candy or some other prize to the winning team. Use the idea of making no mistakes to introduce the topic of failure.

STEP
2

Here Comes the Judge

(Needed: Copies of Repro Resource 4, pencils)

Say: **We're now going to visit "The People's Junior High Court." The junior highers you're going to read about are almost real. The mistakes they've made are totally real. It will be your job as judge to sentence them for their mistakes.**

The sentence may be as easy or as stiff as you think is appropriate. You may even choose to let the offenders go free.

Hand out copies of "The Penalty Fits the Crime" (Repro Resource 4) and pencils. Give your group members a few minutes to read the situations and write their suggested sentences.

After a few minutes, have several group members read their sentences for each scenario.

Afterward, ask: **Do you ever make mistakes? If so, how often?**

What kinds of mistakes are most common for junior highers? Why do you suppose that is?

What's the best way to deal with a mistake after you've made it? Why?

STEP

3

The Big Four

(Needed: Bibles, chalkboard and chalk or newsprint and markers)

Say: **As you can see from the four cases on Repro Resource 4, mistakes can be really serious or they can be really minor. Some mistakes may make you feel dumb, but aren't really wrong. Other mistakes are wrong, and we know it. These mistakes are sin. We're going to learn four simple questions to ask ourselves after a mistake that will help us sort out how we need to respond.**

The first question is "Was it my fault?" Write this question on the board. **Asking this question isn't as easy as it seems because many people often try to put the blame on someone else for their own mistakes. So asking this question requires you to be very honest with yourself. If you really can't figure out if the mistake was your fault or not, pray to God, asking Him to point out whether it was your fault or not.**

If the answer to "Was it my fault?" is yes, then you've already completed the important response by admitting your mistake. Write "Admit your mistake" under the first question on the board.

Cover up what you've written on the board so far. Ask: **What's the first question you should ask yourself after you make a mistake?** ("Was it my fault?")

If the answer is yes, what should you do about it? (Admit your mistake.)

Explain: **The second question is probably the most important one.** Write "Was it sin?" on the board.

Then ask: **What is sin?** Get several responses. If no one mentions it, suggest that sin is anything that goes against what God wants.

Say: **Everyone makes a lot of mistakes. Many of those mistakes are sin and many of them aren't. Let's see if we can tell the difference.**

Read each of the following sentences. Have kids yell out "Yup!" if they think the mistake is a sin and "Nope!" if they think it's not a sin.

   • **I just killed someone.** (Yup!)
   • **I accidentally erased my dad's work report from the computer while trying to log-on to my space game.** (Nope!)
   • **I forgot to do my homework.** (Nope!—assuming it was an honest mistake,)
   • **I told my friend that she's fat.** (Yup!)
   • **I copied one little answer from my fat friend's test.** (Yup!)

Point to the "Was it sin?" question on the board. Ask: **If the answer to this question is yes, what should our response be?** Get several responses. Then write "Ask forgiveness" under the second question on the board.

Cover up everything you've written on the board so far. Ask: **What's the first question you should ask yourself after you make a mistake? If the answer is yes, what should you do about it?**

What's the second question you should ask yourself? If the answer is yes, what should you do about it?

Then explain: **The third question is probably the hardest one. It's also the one a lot of people skip. The question is "Was anyone hurt?"** Write this question on the board.

Then say: **Our mistakes often hurt other people—sometimes physically, but usually emotionally. If someone's been hurt, the best response is to deal with it.** Write "Deal with it" under the third question on the board.

Ask group members to suggest a few examples of how to deal with mistakes that hurt others. (For example, if someone lies to his or her parents, he or she should go back and tell them the truth. Or if someone calls his or her friend a name, he or she should apologize.)

Cover up everything you've written on the board so far. Review all three questions and responses.

Then explain: **The final question is very important. It's the question that decides whether the mistake was completely bad or whether something good can come out of it. The question is "What can I learn from this?"** Write this question on the board.

Say: **Even the worst mistakes can have some positive re-**

sults if we learn from them and change our actions to avoid making similar mistakes in the future.

Take a few minutes to look at two Bible characters—one who didn't learn from his mistake and one who did.

Have group members read Genesis 4:3-8. Then ask: **When God pointed out Cain's mistake in how he gave his offering, how did Cain react?** Some of your group members may reply that Cain went out and killed Abel, but that's jumping the gun. First, Cain got angry. In other words, he wouldn't admit his mistake.

Explain that this was just the beginning of a pretty miserable life for Cain. He never learned to own up to his mistakes. Note that in Genesis 4:9, after God asks Cain about Abel, Cain answers, "Am I my brother's keeper?" He obviously didn't admit his mistake in killing Abel either.

Then have group members turn to Luke 22:54-62. Before reading the passage, ask if anyone knows who Peter was. (He was one of Jesus' disciples.) Have someone read aloud the passage, in which Peter three times denies knowing Jesus.

Ask: **What was Peter's response when he realized his mistake?** (He wept, indicating that he knew he was wrong.) **How was Peter's response different than Cain's?** Get several responses.

Before moving on to the next step, review the four questions on the board one more time.

STEP
4

Practice Makes Perfect

(Needed: Copies of Repro Resource 5, pencils)

Say: **Let's practice using these four questions on a pretend mistake.**

Hand out copies of "Mistake Management" (Repro Resource 5). Your kids should still have pencils from Step 2. Read the "fake mistake" at the top of the sheet; then give group members about two minutes to answer the four questions below. After a couple of minutes, ask several volunteers to share their responses.

Then ask your kids to think of a mistake they've made in the last month or so and write it in the "My Mistake" section on the sheet. When they're finished, have them answer the four questions that follow. Encourage group members to be honest in their responses. Emphasize that no one else will see their sheets.

When everyone is finished, ask for volunteers to share their responses. Do *not* force anyone to share who doesn't want to.

Close the session in prayer, asking God for courage for your group members to confront their mistakes honestly and deal with the results.

THE PENALTY FITS THE Crime

You're the judge for cases involving the following junior high mistakes. What should the penalty be for each one?

MISTAKE #1

Keith's friend James always pinches Keith on the back side of his arm. It hurts a lot and really ticks Keith off. One day, Keith couldn't stand it anymore. After James pinched him, Keith spun around, swore at James, and punched him in the stomach really hard. What should the penalty be?

MISTAKE #2

Teresa's softball team really needs to win some games if they are ever going to make the playoffs. During last week's game, all Teresa had to do to secure a victory for her team was catch the fly ball that came her way. Unfortunately, she dropped the ball, and the other team scored two runs, winning the game. What should the penalty be?

MISTAKE #3

Mike is feeling really guilty. He lied to his parents by telling them he was spending the night at Phil's house. He really went to Alex's house—even though his parents don't allow him to hang out with Alex. Mike and Alex spent the whole night out with some other guys, egging houses and spray painting walls. What should the penalty be?

MISTAKE #4

Cal's chore is to take the trash cans out to the curb every Tuesday night for the Wednesday morning pick-up. He forgot last week, so the cans are totally full. On Wednesday morning, he walks out the front door to go to school and sees the garbage truck driving past his house. He's forgotten again. What should the penalty be?

MISTAKE MANAGEMENT

FAKE MISTAKE

Yesterday you passed along some gossip about one of your friends that wasn't true. Now your friend's pretty bummed at you.

1. Was it my fault?

2. Was it sin?
Action needed:

3. Was anyone hurt?
Action needed:

4. What can I learn from this?

MY MISTAKE:

1. Was it my fault?

2. Was it sin?
Action needed:

3. Was anyone hurt?
Action needed:

4. What can I learn from this?

EXTRA ACTION

Step 1

Have kids form two teams—a "Cops" team and a "Robbers" team. Give each Robber either "stolen money" (a play dollar bill on which you've marked an "S") or "owned money" (a play dollar bill marked with an "O"). Instruct the person to conceal the money on his or her person. At your signal, Cops should chase Robbers from one end of your meeting place to the other. Each Cop who tags a Robber should bring him or her to you. However, only Cops who catch Robbers who happen to have "stolen money" win a prize. Robbers who have been "unjustly" caught with "owned money" win a prize. Everyone else loses. Use this contest to introduce the importance of telling the difference between actions that "break the law" and those that don't. The "real Robbers" (those who had stolen money) are like sins; the "fake robbers" (those with owned money) are like mere mistakes.

Step 3

When you get to the "Yup" and "Nope" statements, designate a corner of your meeting place as "jail." Each time you "confess" to one of the mistakes, kids should drag you in or out of jail according to whether they think you sinned or not. If kids disagree with each other and try to pull you both ways, ask them to explain before they tear you in half.

SMALL GROUP

Step 2

When you get ready to do Repro Resource 4, let your group members decide the penalties for each offense by acting as one of the characters in the scenario. For example, the first scenario would include Keith and James for sure, but remaining group members could assume the roles of friends of both characters, perhaps a teacher who witnessed the punching incident, and anyone else you can think of to plug in to the situation. The second scenario could include Teresa, her friends, and people on the team who are angry at her. In each case, let the participants discuss what the penalty should be. In most cases, they won't reach a consensus, but let them see if they can arrive at a compromise that will satisfy everyone involved.

Step 4

Step 3 is a bit lengthy, so save a little time in Step 4 by having members of your small group work together rather than individually on the "fake mistake" on Repro Resource 5. Let kids talk through the four questions rather than writing down their responses. (They may take notes on their sheets as they talk.) You might also want to personalize the offense described by using names of people in your group. When you get to the personal application of the four questions, you'll want to have kids work individually. Members of a small group can cover a lot of ground effectively by working together; you should allow them to do so whenever it is expedient.

LARGE GROUP

Step 1

Begin the session with a series of activities or games at which all of your kids are bound to fail. You might want to set up several different stations in your meeting area, each one with an almost-impossible task for kids to complete (although the tasks shouldn't seem impossible to your kids). For instance, you might have kids try to stack fifteen dominoes on top of each other vertically. Or you might have kids try to balance a large stack of coins on their elbow and then catch them in their hand. After everyone has had an opportunity to try at least two or three tasks, ask: **How do you feel about failing at these tasks? Why? Are there any other kinds of failure that bother you more? If so, what are they?**

Step 2

For added fun, you might ask a volunteer to play the role of the defendant in each case. As a group, kids should come up with a penalty for each case—a penalty that the defendant (your volunteer) can perform in the meeting area. For instance, for Mistake #4, Cal's penalty may be to pick up all of the trash in your meeting area—after the rest of the group has had a few minutes to spread some litter around.

Step 3

Kids who have discussed moral issues at school may question whether all of the "Yup" and "Nope" statements fall easily into the "sin" and "not sin" categories. For example, if killing is always a sin, what about military service and capital punishment? Is it a sin to tell your friend she's fat if her weight endangers her health? Acknowledge that it may not always be easy to answer the "Was it sin?" question. Point out, however, that instead of avoiding the question, we should get other Christians (pastors, teachers, parents, etc.) to help us sort right from wrong when we aren't sure.

Step 4

Kids who are "old hands" at filling out response sheets like Repro Resource 5 may do so without much thought and without the slightest intention to follow through. You can't force them to take the exercise seriously, but you can offer an incentive (a small prize, for example) for each person who completes the "Action Needed" sections and includes a realistic estimate of how much time would be needed to complete the actions.

Step 3

Have kids form two groups. Let each group look up and discuss one of the Bible passages. Give the groups time to dig as deeply as they can. If possible, try to position an adult leader in each group to ask prompting questions for group members to consider. If your group members don't know the Bible well, it is sometimes better for them to cover one passage thoroughly rather than multiple passages quickly. The group interaction will also challenge them to take responsibility for discovering biblical truth on their own. They can soak up a lot of what you have to say, but they need to interact with Scripture on their own. Give kids the opportunity to do so whenever you can.

Step 4

Make sure that the people in your group know what you mean when you ask if an offense was "sin." Don't assume that they have an accurate definition of the word. At one extreme, some people might equate anything bad (intentional or not) with being sinful. They need to see that bad things happen to people that have nothing to do with sin. At the other extreme is the possibility of assuming that "sin" relates only to the most heinous acts that one can imagine. A white lie or "innocent" gossip is not considered sinful by some people. People at both extremes need to have a more accurate understanding of what sin is.

Step 1

Set up a table with creative materials—modeling clay, paper, pencils, colored markers, and so on. Have kids form pairs. Explain that you want each pair to create something using the materials on the table. However, before you tell them what you want them to create, pretend that you've forgotten something in your office. As you leave, say: **I want the projects completed—and done right—by the time I get back.** Leave the room, giving no further instructions. When you get back, explain to your kids that they were supposed to make a scale model of a nuclear reactor. Express your disappointment at the fact that they didn't do the project "right." Then, coming back to reality, talk with your group about what just happened. Ask: **Have you ever been in a situation in which someone told you that you'd made a terrible mistake when you had no idea that you were doing it? If so, how did that feel?** Allow time for responses. Then say: **God has given us guidelines to help us avoid a whole bunch of mistakes—mistakes that are actually sin. Sometimes, though, mistakes are just mistakes. Today we're going to take a look at how we can tell the difference and how we can respond in either situation.**

Step 4

Have kids refer to what they wrote for "My Mistake" on Repro Resource 5. Then explain that you're going to have a short, impromptu worship service in which kids can bring that mistake to God and ask for forgiveness (if it was a sin), for healing, and for the courage to deal with it. Play some quiet, instrumental music. Encourage kids to pray silently, bringing their mistakes to God. After a short time, pray for all of your group members, that they would be able to deal with their mistakes in a God-honoring fashion.

Step 2

Make the following changes to Repro Resource 4:

• *Mistake #1*—Jenny typically speaks her mind. Today she told Kristi that Kristi's hair looked just terrible. Kristi turned and left in tears. What should the penalty be?

• *Mistake #3*—Pam is feeling really guilty. She lied to her parents by telling them that she was spending the night at Katie's house. She really went to Jennifer's, although her parents don't want her hanging out with Jennifer. They spent the whole night running around with some high school guys that Jennifer knows. What should the penalty be?

• *Mistake #4*—Chris's chore is to keep up with the dishwasher, making sure it's run when full and that clean dishes are put away. But she just hasn't had time lately. Another Monday morning has rolled around with no clean dishes for breakfast. What should the penalty be?

Step 3

For a biblical example of a woman who made a mistake—a very large one—turn to Genesis 3:1-20. Ask for volunteers to read this passage aloud. Then ask: **How did Eve respond when God confronted her with her mistake?** (She totally passed the buck.) **What was the result of her action?** (The ultimate result was that sin entered the world. Also, she and Adam were banished from the garden and their perfect lives became very un-perfect.)

Step 2

Many junior high guys are already experts at dodging responsibility for anything that goes wrong. So before you have your guys establish proper penalties for the offenses on Repro Resource 4, give them an opportunity to demonstrate just how good they are. Read the situations once; then let volunteers act out the roles of the people who made the mistakes. (You'll need to rewrite Mistake #2 with a male character instead of Teresa.) As you go through the situations, ask your volunteers to give excuses for *why* they messed up. In most cases, a good excuse giver can make it seem like someone else is completely at fault for his own mistakes. If your guys are good at this, you'll need to spend some time convincing them to be honest with themselves as they answer the first question in Step 3.

Step 3

Sometimes young people—especially guys—seem to think that Cain got an unfair evaluation from God. After all, he presented an offering just like Abel did. Guys seem to relate to the feeling of being "shafted" even though they're trying to do their best. If this issue comes up in your group, give Cain his "day in court." Assign one person to be Cain, another to be his attorney, and a third person to be Abel's lawyer who is prosecuting for murder. Conduct the trial. Attorneys should present all of the evidence they can find and make their arguments as strong as they can. You should serve as judge so that you can keep all of the facts straight. If no one else mentions it, bring up the fact that Cain is cited in the New Testament for his evil actions, and not the insufficiency of his offering (1 John 3:12).

Step 1

After teams compete to answer the questions provided for them, give them some time to write questions of their own with which they can challenge the other team. Some teams may have more fun writing questions than they do answering them. You need to listen closely to each question, however, to determine whether it's written clearly enough to be answered. Continue the scoring by awarding a point to each question asked that the other team cannot answer. But since so much effort is going into this part of the competition, you might want to award *three* points for each question the other team does answer correctly.

Step 4

You opened the session with questions. You covered four major questions that kids should remember. Now conclude the session with a few more questions, just for fun. Find a copy of *The Kids' Book of Questions* by Gregory Stock (Workman Publishing). It contains 260 opinion questions for young people to consider and answer. For example, here are three to pique your kids' interest:

• "Would you rather be a rich and famous movie star or a great doctor who saves a lot of people but is not wealthy or well known?"

• "Would you be willing to never again get any gifts and surprises if instead you could just ask for anything you wanted and have your parents buy it for you?"

• "If you could live someone else's life for a week—just to see what it would be like—would you want to? If so, who would you pick and why?"

Step 1

Set up a Sega, Nintendo, or interactive CD game in your meeting place. Line kids up, explaining that each person gets fifteen seconds to play, taking up where the last person left off. Continue until everyone's gotten to play at least once. Then ask: **What kinds of mistakes is it possible to make in this game? Is this game very "forgiving" when you make a mistake? How did you feel about mistakes others made before you? When you make mistakes trying something like this, does it make you want to give up, try again, or what?**

Step 4

Instead of using the "fake mistake" from Repro Resource 5, show one of the following video segments (after prescreening it yourself). Have kids apply the Repro Resource 5 questions to the mistake(s) made.
• *Home Alone.* Show early scenes in which Kevin (Macaulay Culkin) is put down by other kids, and then forgotten when his family flies to Paris.
• *Of Mice and Men.* Play the scene in which the mentally slow Lenny (John Malkovich), who has been warned about being careful with a puppy, discovers that he has accidentally killed it.
• *Back to the Future Part II.* Show the scene in which time-traveling Marty McFly (Michael J. Fox), who has been told not to interfere in history, buys a sports almanac that will enable him to win bets on past sporting events.
• *American Graffiti.* Play a scene in which Steve (Ron Howard) and Laurie (Cindy Williams) hurt each other's feelings as they argue about their college plans; or show a scene in which the nerdy Terry (Charles Martin Smith) finds himself drinking and pretending to be someone he isn't.

Step 1

Instead of using the quiz, begin your meeting by making as many mistakes as you can in a minute or so. For example, say **Good morning** if you're meeting in the evening; call a group member by the wrong name; thank another for something that someone else did; give the wrong date for an upcoming event (be sure to correct it later); etc. When kids notice your mistakes, deny that you've made any. Have a volunteer (with whom you've arranged this beforehand) persist in pointing out your errors; then you get angry, walk over to the person, and pretend to strangle him or her to death. Then regain your composure, claim that you don't make mistakes, and move on to Step 2. Before getting into serious discussion, thank your volunteer. Then ask: **How do you feel about people who make mistakes? How do you feel about people who won't admit their mistakes? Why?**

Step 3

Instead of studying the stories of Cain and Peter, read and discuss Proverbs 6:1-5. Explain that the mistake referred to here was taking responsibility for somebody else's debt—which at the time could end in slavery. Ask: **According to these verses, what should you do if you've made a mistake?** (Humble yourself; undo right away what you've done.) **Why be humble?** (If you won't admit that you've made a mistake, you can't learn from it or undo it.) **Why hurry?** (Some mistakes have dangerous results; the longer you wait, the easier it is to pretend things will work out by themselves.) In Step 4, skip the top half of Repro Resource 5 and just have kids work on the "My Mistake" section.

Step 1

Play a couple of segments from a sports "bloopers" video compilation. If possible, try to find a segment that shows a very popular athlete (perhaps Michael Jordan or Deion Sanders) making a mistake. Afterward, ask: **How do you think _____ felt about making that mistake? How do you think he (or she) reacted? Why do you think he (or she) reacted in that way? What can we learn from _____'s attitude toward making a mistake?**

Step 2

Add the following scenario to Repro Resource 4:
• *Mistake #5*—Ramon knows that his best friend was involved in vandalizing a school classroom over the weekend. On Monday, the principal asks Ramon if he knows anything about the vandalism. Ramon says no, lying to protect his friend. What should the penalty be?

Step 2

Make the following changes to Repro Resource 4:

• *Mistake #3*—Mike lied to his parents by telling them that he spent the night at Phil's house. He actually went to Alex's house, where there was a huge party—several kegs, lots of people, and no parents. Mike drank so much that he got sick. What should the penalty be?

• *Mistake #4*—Cal's chore is to keep the car, which he uses quite a bit, filled with gas and clean. He hasn't washed it for two weeks, and the gas tank is almost on empty. He figures that he'll take care of it on Saturday. However, on Friday morning, Cal's mom tells him that she and her prayer group are going to visit several nursing homes, and that she's taking the car. What should Cal's penalty be?

Step 3

Point out that another thing we need to learn about mistakes—besides how to deal with ones that we make—is how to deal with mistakes other people make that affect us. Spend a few minutes talking about how we typically respond when someone's mistake affects us (we get angry), and what we could do to change or respond differently, using Christ as our model. Jesus typically confronted people with their mistakes—usually gently, but sometimes with anger (with the money changers in the temple, for example). He always responded with love, and He always forgave.

Step 1

Have kids form two teams. Let the teams take turns giving each other challenges, trying to "stump" the other team. For example, a team might challenge its opponents to make ten straight shots—using a paper wad and a trash can—without a miss in under two minutes. If a team cannot meet the challenge issued by the other team, the challenging team gets a chance to meet the challenge. If the challenging team can meet its own challenge after its opponents have failed, it gets a point. The team with the most points at the end of the game is the winner. Of course, there will be some failure as teams try to meet their challenges, so this activity can serve as an introduction to the topic of the session.

Step 2

Read the description of Abraham Lincoln found on page 11 of this book (in Wayne Rice's article "If at First You Don't Succeed . . ."). See if your group members can guess who you're talking about. Afterward, ask: **What's the worst failure you've ever experienced?** Be prepared to share your own worst failure with the group. Then ask: **What can we learn from Abraham Lincoln about dealing with failure?**

Date Used:

Approx. Time

Step 1: No Mistakes Allowed _____

o Extra Action
o Large Group
o Fellowship & Worship
o Extra Fun
o Media
o Short Meeting Time
o Urban
o Sixth Grade
Things needed:

Step 2: Here Comes the Judge _____

o Small Group
o Large Group
o Mostly Girls
o Mostly Guys
o Urban
o Combined Junior High/High School
o Sixth Grade
Things needed:

Step 3: The Big Four _____

o Extra Action
o Heard It All Before
o Little Bible Background
o Mostly Girls
o Mostly Guys
o Short Meeting Time
o Combined Junior High/High School
Things needed:

Step 4: Practice Makes Perfect _____

o Small Group
o Heard It All Before
o Little Bible Background
o Fellowship & Worship
o Extra Fun
o Media
Things needed:

Friendly Fire

YOUR GOALS FOR THIS SESSION:

Choose one or more

☐ To help kids recognize that pride is the source of almost all quarrels.

☐ To help kids understand that sometimes we need to give up our "rights" in order to fix friendship fights.

☐ To help kids choose one "right" to give up for friendship.

☐ Other _____

_____

Your Bible Base:

Genesis 13:1-12
Proverbs 13:10

Sumo Pillow Fight

(Needed: Masking tape, two pillows, prizes [optional])

Before the session, use masking tape to make a circle approximately four feet in diameter in the middle of your floor. As group members arrive, divide them into two teams. Explain that the teams will be competing in sumo pillow fights. Have each team choose a contestant for the first battle. Give each contestant a pillow. Explain that the object of the game is to push your opponent out of the circle. However, the contestants may only touch each other with the pillows. Both contestants must grasp their pillows with both hands during the entire battle. The first contestant to step on or over the line is out. The winner of each round scores one point for his or her team. Continue the game until everyone has had the opportunity to do battle at least twice. Afterward, you may want to award small prizes to the winning team.

Use the sumo pillow fight activity to introduce the topic of "battling" with friends. Ask: **How often would you say you get into minor arguments with your friends?** Get several responses.

How often would you say you get into major fights with your friends? Again get several responses.

Friction Fuel

(Needed: Copies of Repro Resource 6, pencils)

Hand out copies of "Friction Fuel" (Repro Resource 6) and pencils. Explain that the sheet contains a list of several items that might cause conflict between friends. Two of the items have been left blank for group members to fill in their own suggestions. After group members have come up with a couple of additional ideas, have them rank the items from 1 to 18 according to how likely they are to cause a fight between friends (with "1" being "most likely to cause a fight" and "18"

being "least likely to cause a fight"). Give kids a few minutes to complete the sheet. When everyone is finished, ask several volunteers to share and explain their rankings. If you have time, you might want to periodically ask for real-life examples of when one of the items on the sheet caused a conflict between a group member and his or her friend. Be prepared to share a couple of examples yourself.

After you've gone through the sheet and several volunteers have shared their responses, ask: **So what's the number one cause for fights between friends?**

After you've gotten several responses, say: **Let's take a look at what the Bible says is one of the major causes of conflicts and quarrels.**

STEP 3

The Problem of Pride

(Needed: Bibles)

Have group members read Proverbs 13:10. Then ask: **According to this verse, what is one of the roots of quarreling?** (Pride.)

What is pride? Group members will probably offer several definitions and may focus on the idea of being proud of something. If no one mentions it, suggest that pride is false confidence that you're right or that your way is the best (or only) way.

Then ask: **How might pride cause conflict between friends?** (Fighting usually results from two people wanting their own way.)

Explain that you're going to be looking at the biblical story of Abram to get an idea of how to handle conflict between friends. Have group members turn in their Bibles to Genesis 13:1-12. Ask a couple of volunteers to read the passage aloud. In this passage, Abram and Lot and their herdsmen are quarreling because they have too many people and animals living on the same piece of land. Abram, the uncle of Lot, had the right to choose whatever land he wanted. He could have sent Lot packing. Instead, he gives up his right and allows Lot to choose the land that he wants.

After reading the passage, ask: **What was causing the conflict between Abram and Lot?** (There wasn't enough land to allow both of their herds to graze.)

As Lot's uncle, living in a culture in which older relatives had tons of authority, what could Abram have done in this

situation? (He could have decided what land he wanted and told Lot to get lost.)

What did Abram do instead? (He allowed Lot to choose first which land he wanted.)

What is a right? (No, we're not talking about the opposite of a wrong! A right is something you deserve.)

What are some rights we have in this country? (The right of free speech, the right to worship as we desire, etc.)

What are some rights we might expect in a friendship? This may be a hard question for your group members to answer. If so, get them started with suggestions like the right to be listened to and the right to expect honesty.

Then ask: **If pride is one of the major causes of conflict between friends, what can we learn from Abram's example about solving quarrels?** (Sometimes it may be necessary to give up some of your rights in order to solve or avoid a conflict.)

How hard is it to give up your rights? (For many people, it's really, really, really hard.) If no one mentions it, point out that Jesus gave up His heavenly rights in order to become a human being and die for us.

STEP 4

The Bill of Rights

(Needed: Copies of Repro Resource 7, pencils)

Hand out copies of "The Friendship Bill of Rights" (Repro Resource 7). Your group members should still have their small wooden destructive devices (better known as pencils) from Step 2. Let kids work in small groups to list as many "friendship rights" as they can think of. After a few minutes, ask each group to share its answers. As each group shares, instruct the other group members to pay attention, adding any rights to their sheets that their group didn't come up with.

After all of the groups have shared, ask: **Which of the rights on your sheet would be easy for you to give up? Why?** Get several responses.

Then ask: **Which of the rights on your sheet would be hard for you to give up? Why?** Again get several responses.

Ask several group members to choose one friendship right listed on their sheet and explain how giving up that right might solve or prevent a conflict between friends. Encourage kids to use real-life examples when

OPTIONS

EXTRA ACTION

SMALL GROUP

HEARD IT ALL BEFORE

LITTLE BIBLE BACKGROUND

FELLOWSHIP & WORSHIP

MOSTLY GIRLS

possible. You should be prepared to share at least one example yourself.

As you wrap up the session, ask group members to circle one friendship right on Repro Resource 7 that would be very difficult for them to give up. Explain that circling that right indicates a desire to try to give up that right in order to avoid or solve a conflict with a friend.

After a few minutes, close the session in prayer, thanking God for the gift of friendships and asking Him to give your group members the strength and courage to give up certain friendship rights for the sake of maintaining peace with friends.

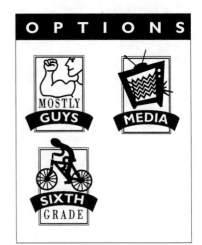

FRICTION FUEL

Number the following items from 1 to 18 according to how likely they are to cause a fight between friends (1 = "most likely to cause a fight between friends"; 18 = "least likely to cause a fight between friends"). You'll need to fill in two of the blanks with ideas of your own.

___ RULES

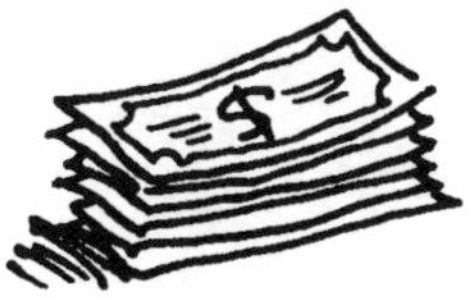

___ **Borrowing stuff**

___ *Spending too much time together*

__ **Money**

___ Deciding which video to rent

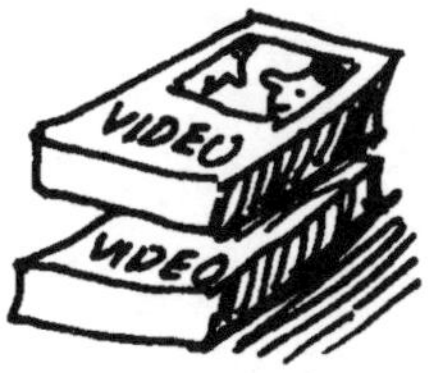
VIDEO
VIDEO

___ Other friends

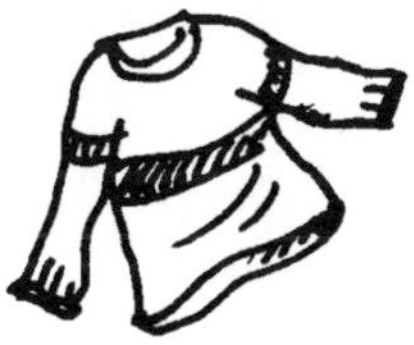

___ **Boyfriend/girlfriend**

___ **Lies**

____ *Clothes*

___ **Put downs**

__ *Busy schedules*

___ Deciding how to spend your time

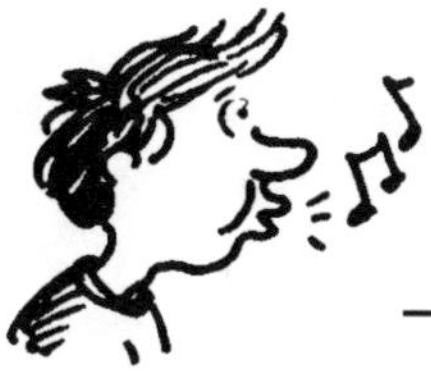

___ ANNOYING HABITS

__ Bossiness

___ **Not talking**

___ Other ____________________

___ Gossip

___ Other ____________________

The Friendship Bill of Rights

With my close friends, I have the right to expect the following:

1.

2.

3.

4.

5.

6.

7.

8.

9.

10.

11.

12.

Step 2

Have kids form small groups. Give each group a copy of Repro Resource 6, a pair of scissors, a strong refrigerator magnet, and a steel surface (folding chair, coffee can, etc.). Have the groups cut the eighteen items from the sheet. Each group should experiment to see how many of the items can be placed between the magnet and the metal before the magnet no longer sticks to the metal. Each group should then put that number of slips, choosing only the "top friendship breakers," between the magnet and the metal. Go from group to group, finding out which items kids chose. Afterward, discuss how these friendship-breakers can cause friends to lose their "attraction." Ask: **How many things can come between friends before the friends no longer stick together?**

Step 4

Establish a "trading post" at the front or back of your meeting place. Have each person come to the trading post and "give up" one or more rights (which he or she has torn from Repro Resource 7) in exchange for a "friend-ship"—a small plastic toy boat. Let kids take their boats home as a reminder that not insisting on having one's way can help keep a friendship afloat.

Step 1

Before the session, arrange to have a few kids fake a serious argument with each other. Toward the end of the sumo pillow fight, one person might accuse another of cheating. That person might then accuse the first person of lying. A friend or two might then take up for each of the feuding parties. The fight should culminate with one of the "sides" deciding, "We just can't stay for a meeting with a cheater like him. We're walking home!" The other side might then determine, "We're sorry. We're just in no mood to meet. We've got to leave too." See how the remaining group members react. In addition to the emotional turmoil that is caused, kids should quickly see that unsettled conflict can seriously damage "group dynamics." After a couple of minutes, your actors should return. As you continue the session, kids should have in mind the especially destructive potential of conflicts among members of a small group.

Step 4

Have kids work together to compile "The Friendship Bill of Rights." As they come up with ideas, write a master list on the board. After you've compiled the list, have kids prioritize the rights as a group. You won't be able to be precise about the preferred order, but it doesn't matter. If everyone agrees that one thing is very important, put it at the top of the list. If kids agree that something isn't important, stick it at the end. When kids disagree, put those things in the middle. Type up the master list and make copies of it to hand out at your next meeting. At that time, review what you discussed during this session and ask group members to post their list of "rights" in places where they will see them frequently

Step 1

With a large group, you might want to expand the sumo pillow fights. You'll need to bring in two mattresses. Divide kids into teams of four, making sure that each team has a mix of large and small kids. Tape off a large area in your room to serve as a "battleground." Bring two teams into the battleground at a time. Assign each team a mattress. Explain that team members must stand behind their mattress, holding on to its edges. The object of the game is to push (using only the mattress) your opponents out of the battleground area. The team that pushes its opponents out of the battleground area wins the match and advances to the next round. Continue until only one team remains. Afterward, use the activity to introduce the topic of "battling" with friends.

Step 2

Have kids form teams. Instruct each team to come up with a scenario in which famous friends get into a fight. For instance, one team might come up with a scenario in which Fred Flintstone and Barney Rubble get into an argument about who's the better driver (Fred: "My feet are bigger, so I can stop the car faster"). Another team might come up with a scenario in which the Lone Ranger and Tonto get into a fight about their horses (Tonto: "Just once, I'd like to say 'Hi ho, Silver, away!'"). After a few minutes, have each team describe or (even better) act out its scenario. Then move on to the Repro Resource 6 activity.

Step 3

If kids associate the story of Abram and Lot with their flannelgraph days, you may find it hard to get them to consider it anew. Instead, study these passages on the causes of quarrels: II Timothy 2:23, 24 (stupid arguments; resentment); James 4:1-3 (wanting what we can't have; not asking God for what we want); I Corinthians 3:1-3 (being spiritual babies; jealousy). You might also look at these passages on ways to "bounce back" from quarrels: Proverbs 15:1, 18 (give gentle answers; be patient); Proverbs 26:20 (don't gossip about problems you're having with a friend); Ephesians 4:26, 27, 29-32 (start working on your problem quickly instead of letting it grow; say things that build each other up; be kind, compassionate, forgiving).

Step 4

With today's emphasis on the rights of children, some kids may have been taught at school and elsewhere that they should be careful to guard their rights, and not give them up. Avoid giving the impression that people really have no rights, or that kids should give up all of their rights for the sake of keeping friendships intact. For example, kids should not let "friends" abuse them physically, use them sexually, pressure them into doing wrong, or endanger them. Point out that true friends wouldn't do these things anyway. The main right we should be willing to give up is the "right" to always have our own way.

Step 3

The Abram and Lot story is a good example of yielding one's rights for the good of a relationship. But if your kids don't know much about the Bible, it may be better to focus on the general principle of yielding rights rather than on one specific instance. An excellent reference that will apply to many different personal struggles is Jesus' Sermon on the Mount (Matthew 5–7). During the session, focus specifically on Matthew 5:38-48. Show your kids the high standards that Jesus sets for His followers. Explain that when people learn to do what Jesus instructs, they find peace of mind that others will never know. Encourage your kids to read through the rest of the Sermon on the Mount (in reasonable increments) during the next week or so. It's a good starting place for people trying to find out what Christianity is all about.

Step 4

If your kids are like most people, they'll insist that what you're saying isn't fair. If so, ask: **Do you think the world would be a better place if everything were always absolutely fair? Would you want to be punished every single time you did something wrong? Or would you rather have time to think about what you'd done and then ask forgiveness?** Differentiate between *justice* (eye-for-an-eye fairness), *mercy* (not being punished for something we deserve to be punished for), and *grace* (receiving positive gifts that we don't deserve and could never earn on our own). Explain that God is absolutely just, but because Jesus has sacrificed Himself for our sins, God can also be merciful and gracious to us. And since we receive God's mercy and grace in abundance, we should willingly pass it on to other people who offend *us* from time to time.

Step 1

Have kids form teams of three or four. Give each team a stack of magazines or other printed materials that contain advertisements. Give the teams two assignments: (1) Find as many ads as possible that encourage people to "watch out for number one." (2) Find as many ads as possible that show people sacrificing for the good of someone else or giving to someone else. Award prizes to the team that finds the most appropriate ads. Then say: **Our society is very focused on "watching out for number one," which develops proud, selfish people. What do you think are some results of pride and selfishness?** If no one mentions it, suggest that fighting is a result.

Step 4

Use the following activity to help kids take the focus off themselves and put it on God and others. Give each person a piece of paper and a pencil. Instruct kids to make two columns on the sheet. Say: **In the first column, write as many good things as you can think of about your best friend. In the second column, write as many good things as you can think of about God.** Allow kids a few minutes to work. Then encourage kids to spend some time in prayer, thanking God for creating a friend with so many good attributes and offering adoration to Him for His own attributes.

Step 3

After looking at Abram's example of conflict resolution in Genesis 13, present your girls with the following scenario and discuss possible positive ways to resolve it. Say: **Annie borrowed Mary Jane's favorite sweater to wear to the fall dance. Annie kept forgetting to return it to Mary Jane. When she finally returned it a month later, the sweater smelled like smoke. Both of Annie's parents smoke. What should Mary Jane do?**

Step 4

After your girls have completed Repro Resource 7 and have shared their responses, ask them to think of a recent quarrel they've had. Say: **In that situation, which of these rights could you have given up to avoid the quarrel? How might that have changed the outcome?** After a few minutes, ask volunteers to share their stories and solutions. Be ready with an example of your own, if possible.

Step 2

Before your guys fill out Repro Resource 6, try to get some true stories out of them. Some guys are likely to take pride in some of their previous battles. And since you're going to address the topic of pride in Step 3, this is where you can "set up" your guys. For each category listed on Repro Resource 6, try to find at least one person willing to talk about a time when that specific thing led to a disagreement or fight with someone. Your guys may be surprised to see how many things they can "person-alize." After seeing how real some of these things are, have kids begin to prioritize the likelihood of each thing causing a disagreement.

Step 4

You should probably address the issue of "manliness" if you're telling your guys to give up their rights in order to avoid an argument. Teenage culture says to stand up for your rights. Guys are especially likely to feel uncomfortable if they voluntarily allow others to take advantage of them. Before you close the session, ask: **What do you think other people will think about you if they see you give up something to stay out of a fight? Do you care what other people think as long as you feel good about yourself? Can you walk away from a fight and feel good about yourself? Does it take more strength to let someone else have his way in an argument, or to get into a fight about it? Why? Should you always yield your rights to other people? If not, what guidelines can you use to know when to let go and when to stand fast?**

Step 1

After the sumo pillow fight, but before you explain the topic of the session, pull out a nicely wrapped gift. Explain that "a fine prize" is in the package, and that the team who is in possession of the gift when you give the signal will get to keep it. Then begin a keep-away game of sorts, using the teams already established for the pillow fight. Short of inflicting physical harm on one another, participants should make an anything-goes effort to get the package. After possession has changed hands several times, give a signal to stop. Let the winners open their prize. Inside should be something that is sure to be a letdown for the winners (a nickel, a picture of you, or whatever). Explain that many times we fight extremely hard to maintain our "rights," only to realize too late that our efforts were all but wasted.

Step 2

On individual slips of paper, write out the list of things that cause fights between friends (from Repro Resource 6). Call two volunteers at a time to the front of the room. Let them draw one of the slips and *immediately* begin an impromptu fight over that topic. If you wish, have some prizes ready for the people who do the best job. You may be surprised at how quickly some of these things can generate some intense feelings. Even though the volunteers won't actually be fighting, they will draw from times in the past when these items were genuine sources of friction in their relationships.

Step 2

Instead of having kids rank the items on Repro Resource 6, show a couple of the following video clips (after prescreening them yourself). Have kids mark any of the eighteen items on the sheet that apply to the relationships depicted in the scenes. Let kids add items to the list as needed.

• *Teenage Mutant Ninja Turtles.* Show a scene in which the personalities of the sewer-bred dudes clash.

• *The Three Stooges.* Play a scene in which the Stooges get on each other's nerves (and possibly your own).

• *Grumpy Old Men.* Show one of the many scenes in which longtime acquaintances played by Jack Lemmon and Walter Matthau display their inability to get along.

• *Planes, Trains, and Automobiles.* Play a scene in which the uptight Neal (Steve Martin) is forced to travel with the tiresome Del (John Candy).

Step 4

As kids work on Repro Resource 7, play a contemporary Christian song that points out how Jesus gave up His rights for our sake. Possibilities include "The Coloring Song" (Petra), "Why" (Michael Card), "Man in the Middle" (Wayne Watson), and "Forgiven" (David Meece).

Step 1

Skip Step 1. In Step 2, have kids form pairs. Give each pair a copy of Repro Resource 6. Explain that the members of each pair have two minutes to rank the eighteen items. The partners should work together, trying to reach a consensus on how the items should be ranked. Then, instead of having kids share how they ranked all eighteen items, just ask about #1 and #18. Ask: **Was this activity frustrating? If so, how? Did you argue? Did one person always give in to the other? What do you do in real life when you and a friend disagree? How do you keep your friendship together when you don't agree?**

Step 3

Instead of studying Abram and Lot, a story which requires background explanation, look at the familiar parable of the prodigal son (Luke 15:11-32). Discuss how the father forgave the son and took him back, even though pride could have kept the father from doing so. Note that pride could have kept the son from returning too. Call attention to the elder son as an example of a person who insists on his rights and won't make peace with someone who doesn't "deserve" it. In Step 4, instead of having kids try to come up with friendship rights, write your own on Repro Resource 7 before copying it. (Examples might include the following: "Friends have the right to know each other's secrets"; "Friends have the right to expect never to be put down by each other"; "Friends have to the right to eat off each other's plates"; "Friends have the right to expect presents from each other on birthdays"; "Friends have the right to be late without being criticized for it.") Discuss the sheet as time allows.

Step 2

Rather than using Repro Resource 6, ask kids to brainstorm a list of comments that might cause an argument or fight between friends. Comments might include things like "When are you going to pay me the money you owe me?" and "Were you flirting with my girlfriend [or boyfriend]?" After kids have listed several such comments, discuss as a group what kinds of situations are most likely to cause conflict between friends. Perhaps you could make a top-ten list of your kids' responses. When you're finished, move on to Step 3.

Step 3

Ask group members to share some examples of arguments between friends that escalated into major conflicts, perhaps resulting in longtime feuds or even physical violence. Some of your kids will probably be aware of such situations in their neighborhood. If possible, be prepared to share an example of your own. Ask: **What might the two friends have done to prevent the situation from reaching a boiling point? Why do you suppose they didn't do it?** Use your discussion to introduce what the Bible says about conflict and quarreling.

Step 2

After group members have completed Repro Resource 6, list the items on the board. Then ask your high schoolers: **Do any of these items, or the order in which you ranked them, change between junior high and high school? If so, explain.** Allow time for discussion. Point out that though some of the specific reasons for fighting may change, the one element (pride) that is behind them all doesn't change—whether you're in junior high, high school, or you're an adult.

Step 3

As you're discussing the issue of pride, ask: **What's the difference between being proud and having a healthy self-esteem? Is having a healthy self-image biblical?** Encourage several kids to respond. Then point out that pride, as mentioned in Step 3, is the false confidence that you're right and that your way is the only or best way. Pride leaves no room for God. Having a healthy self-esteem or self-image is knowing that we are children of God, that we are loved eternally by Him, and that our accomplishments are achieved with His strength. It's feeling good about who we are and what we do because of who God is and what He's done for us. It's viewing ourselves through His eyes.

Step 1

If you're concerned that the sumo pillow fight might get out of hand with your sixth graders, try a different opener. Have kids form pairs. Give each pair a large rubber band. If possible, make sure that all of the rubber bands are of the same size and strength. Explain that the pairs will be competing to see which one can stretch its rubber band furthest before it breaks. You'll need a yardstick or some other measuring device to determine which rubber band gets stretched furthest. Award prizes to the winning pair. Use this activity to introduce the idea that sometimes friendships get "stretched" and face more tension when conflicts arise. If the conflicts aren't handled properly, the friendship might "break."

Step 4

As you wrap up the session, give your kids an opportunity to write a note to a friend with whom they've had a conflict. In their notes, kids should incorporate some of the principles you talked about in the session. Explain that the purpose of the note is to restore a friendship or to resolve a conflict that's starting to cause some problems. After a few minutes, close the session in prayer. As kids leave, encourage them to deliver their notes.

Date Used:

Approx.
Time

Step 1: Sumo Pillow Fight _____
o Small Group
o Large Group
o Fellowship & Worship
o Extra Fun
o Short Meeting Time
o Sixth Grade
Things needed:

Step 2: Friction Fuel _____
o Extra Action
o Large Group
o Mostly Guys
o Extra Fun
o Media
o Urban
o Combined Junior High/High School
Things needed:

Step 3: The Problem of Pride _____
o Heard It All Before
o Little Bible Background
o Mostly Girls
o Short Meeting Time
o Urban
o Combined Junior High/High School
Things needed:

Step 4: The Bill of Rights _____
o Extra Action
o Small Group
o Heard It All Before
o Little Bible Background
o Fellowship & Worship
o Mostly Girls
o Mostly Guys
o Media
o Sixth Grade
Things needed:

SESSION

4 "I Did It"

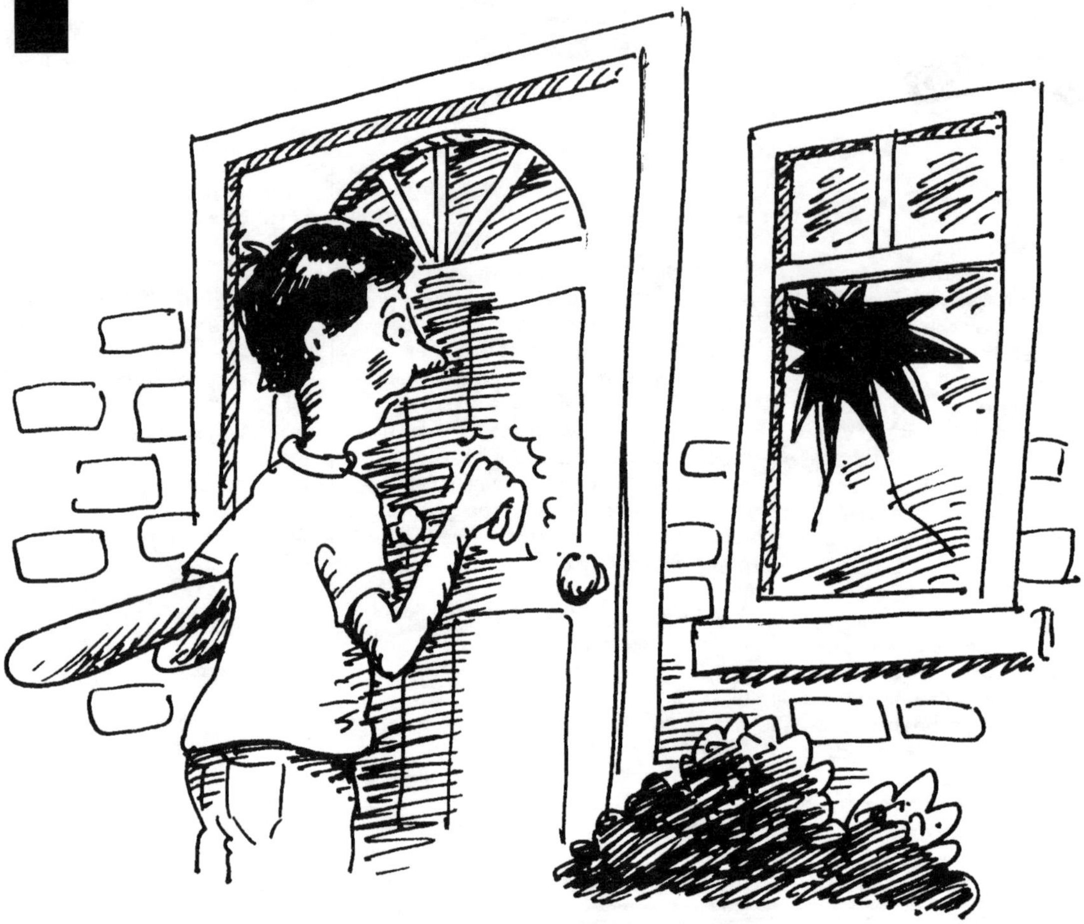

YOUR GOALS FOR THIS SESSION:

Choose one or more

- [ ] To help kids see how David took responsibility for his actions.
- [ ] To help kids understand that taking responsibility for their actions is part of growing up.
- [ ] To help kids practice making decisions and projecting the consequences of those decisions.
- [ ] Other ______________________________

Your Bible Base:

II Samuel 11:2-17;
12:1-10, 13

It's Your Choice

(Needed: Cut-apart copy of Repro Resource 8, prizes)

OPTIONS

SMALL GROUP

LARGE GROUP

FELLOWSHIP & WORSHIP

EXTRA FUN

MEDIA

SHORT MEETING TIME

SIXTH GRADE

As group members arrive, have them form four teams. Before the session, you'll need to cut apart a copy of "Share It, Do It, Sound Like It, or Give It" (Repro Resource 8). Place the cut-apart cards in four stacks—"Share It," "Do It," "Sound Like It," and "Give It"—at the front of the room. Explain that the activity is very simple. One at a time, each team will send a contestant to the front of the room. That person will draw a card from one of the stacks and then follow the instructions on the card. If the person carries out the assignment wholeheartedly, with excitement and enthusiasm (you'll be the judge), his or her team gets a point. If the person carries out the assignment halfheartedly, his or her team gets a half point. If the person refuses to carry out the assignment, his or her team loses a point. Continue until everyone in the group has had an opportunity to draw a card or until all of the cards have been drawn. The team with the most points at the end of the game is the winner. Award prizes (perhaps a bag of candy) to the members of the winning team.

Afterward, ask: **Who decided whether you would carry out the instructions on the card(s) you drew?** Most group members will probably agree that ultimately, the decision was theirs. Use this activity to introduce the topic of taking responsibility for one's own actions.

The Mouse Test

(Needed: Two signs)

Ask: **How many of you have heard the expression "Are you a man or a mouse?"** Get a show of hands.
What do you think the expression means? If no one mentions

it, suggest that the expression usually refers to someone who's kind of wimpy about taking responsibility for his actions.

Explain: **I'm going to describe several junior highers. I want you to decide whether their actions make them a mouse or a man—or woman.**

Before the session, you'll need to make two signs—one that says "Mouse" and one that says "Man/Woman." Tape the signs on opposite walls of your room. Have your group members stand up. Explain that after you read a description, they should move toward the sign that best represents the character. The descriptions are as follows (feel free to add some of your own):

• **Mike threw a baseball through the front window of his house and blamed it on his little brother. Mouse or man?**

• **Janice ate the last piece of cake in the refrigerator without realizing that it was her brother's. To make up for it, she bought him some Hostess Cupcakes at the supermarket. Mouse or woman?**

• **Marcella borrowed her friend's sweater and then lost it. She never mentioned it to her friend, who seems to have forgotten about the sweater. Mouse or woman?**

• **Tyrone chose to go camping with some friends rather than play in the last baseball game of the season. He called his coach a week in advance to let him know about his plans. Mouse or man?**

• **Thomas was talking in church during the sermon when an old woman in front of him turned around and asked him to be quiet. Thomas whispered, "I wasn't talking." Mouse or man?**

• **Jennifer totally forgot to do her homework. She admitted to her teacher that she forgot to do it and then asked for a one-day extension. Mouse or woman?**

Ask volunteers to explain their responses for each scenario.

OPTIONS

HEARD IT ALL BEFORE

MOSTLY GUYS

JR. HIGH / HIGH SCHOOL COMBINED

SIXTH GRADE

STEP 3

Response-o-rama

(Needed: Bibles)

Ask: **Why do you think some people often aren't willing to take responsibility for their actions?** (Perhaps it's because they

don't want to face the consequences for their actions—or at least what they think the consequences might be.)

What are some ways that people avoid taking responsibility for their actions? (Lie about it, make an excuse, pretend it never happened, blame someone else.)

Explain: **We're going to look at someone in the Bible who made some huge mistakes, and we're going to focus on how he responded to those mistakes. The name of this great mistake maker is David.**

Ask group members to turn in their Bible to II Samuel 11. Have someone read aloud verses 2-17. Afterward, ask: **What were David's mistakes here?** (He committed adultery. He tried to cover up his adultery with deceit. He had Uriah killed.)

Have someone read aloud II Samuel 12:1-10. But don't let group members read David's reaction to Nathan yet. Have kids reassemble into the teams they formed in Step 1. Assign each team one of the following possible responses of David. Instruct the members of each team to consider what David might say to Nathan based on their assigned response. Then have each team choose two representatives, who will play the roles of Nathan and David, to act out the response for the rest of the group.

The four possible responses are as follows:

1. David blames someone else for everything he did.
2. David makes up an excuse for what he did.
3. David tries to ignore what he did.
4. David takes responsibility for his actions.

Give the teams about five minutes to work. During this time, walk around the room, offering help to those who need it. When everyone is finished, have each team present its scenario.

After all four scenarios have been performed, read aloud II Samuel 12:13. Explain that David's remorse for his actions is well documented in the Bible. In fact, one of David's psalms—Psalm 51—deals with David's great sorrow as a result of this incident. David also took responsibility for Bathsheba from that point on.

Face the Consequences

(Needed: Copies of Repro Resource 9, pencils)

Explain: **Part of growing up is learning how to take responsibility for your actions. The most immature adults are usually the ones who try to pass off their actions as someone else's fault or the ones who are always making excuses for the things they do. People who won't take responsibility for their actions often have a hard time in the adult world.**

Part of the solution is thinking about the consequences of your choices before you make them, and then deciding if you're willing to accept those consequences. If you're not willing to face the consequences of a decision, it might be wise to make a different choice. Let's look at some examples of this.

Hand out copies of "Take the Consequences" (Repro Resource 9) and pencils. Read the first situation aloud. Have group members write down what they would do in that situation and what the consequences of their actions might be. Then read the follow-up scenario and have group members write down what they would do in that situation and what the consequences might be. When everyone is finished, ask several volunteers to share what they wrote. Let other group members suggest consequences that the volunteers may not have considered. Continue with the second situation on the sheet in the same way.

As you wrap up the session, encourage your group members to start considering consequences before they make decisions. Then close in prayer, asking God for courage for your group members to take responsibility for their actions.

Share It, Do It, Sound Like It, or Give It

Share It	Do It	Sound Like It	Give It
Share something about yourself that no one else in this room knows.	Do an Elvis impersonation.	Sound like a rap artist.	Give someone of the opposite sex your phone number.
Share the name of someone you like.	Do an impression of a famous celebrity singing the national anthem.	Sound like a top-40 radio DJ.	Give someone some money.
Share your favorite color.	Do a square dance.	Sound like a squealing pig.	Give someone a hug.
Share something embarrassing that has happened to you.	Do an impression of a bodybuilder in competition.	Sound like Barney the Dinosaur.	Give someone a back rub.
Share a funny joke.	Do twenty-five jumping jacks.	Sound like a chicken laying an egg.	Give someone a pat on the back.
Share the name you'd pick for yourself if you were the opposite gender.	Do an impression of a ballerina giving a performance.	Sound like a horror movie.	Give someone a suggestion.

TAKE THE CONSEQUENCES

SITUATION 1

You sit next to this kid in science class who is really annoying. He's always passing you notes and whispering to you while the teacher's talking. Today, for the very first time ever, you send a note back responding to his note. The teacher sees you and asks, "Are you passing notes in my class?"

What do you do?

What might some of the consequences of that choice be?

Follow-up
The teacher calls your parents that night and tells them she caught you passing notes in class. After your dad hangs up the phone, he looks at you and asks, "What do you have to say for yourself?"

What do you do?

What might some of the consequences of that choice be?

SITUATION 2

You have a ton of homework due tomorrow. But your friend's having a killer party tonight.

What do you do?

What might some of the consequences of that choice be?

Follow-up
You went to the party and didn't touch your history reading assignment. Now your teacher springs a pop quiz on you.

What do you do?

What might some of the consequences of that choice be?

Step 3

After reading II Samuel 11:2-17 and summarizing David's sins, have kids form two teams—the Cover-up Team and the Uncovering Team. Give the Cover-up Team three smelly items—a plate of fresh, chopped garlic; a cup of vinegar-soaked cotton balls; and a bowl of diced onions. Give this team a spray can of air freshener too. The Cover-up Team's job is to hide the smelly items in your meeting place and to use up to three two-second squirts of air freshener to throw the other team off the track. Send the Uncovering Team out of the room while the hiding and spraying are done. Then bring in the Uncovering Team to search. If the search takes more than three minutes, the Cover-up Team wins. If not, the Uncovering Team wins. Then ask: **How is sin like the smelly things we hid? How do we try to cover up our sins? Does it really work?** Then proceed with the rest of David's story in II Samuel 12:1-10.

Step 4

Have kids stand in a circle. Give one person a dollar. Instruct him or her to pass the dollar to the next person in the circle, who will pass it to the next person, and so on. Point out that this is "passing the buck." Make sure kids understand that this means "avoiding responsibility." Then point at someone in the circle and say, **The buck stops here!** The person holding the dollar must keep it—and answer the questions for the first part of Situation 1 on Repro Resource 9. (If you wish, give the buck-holder the option of paying someone else to answer the question.) Make sure kids understand that "The buck stops here" refers to accepting personal responsibility. Repeat the buck-passing, the buck-stopping, and the answering for the rest of the questions on the sheet.

Step 1

A small group seldom has the luxury of forming four teams. So instead of having kids form teams, randomly number the squares on Repro Resource 8. Then ask each person to give you a number between 1 and 24. Kids must perform the action in the square with the number they chose in it. Be sure to announce the category for each action: Share It, Do It, Sound Like It, or Give It. Don't bother keeping score; the activity will be fun enough in itself.

Step 3

Again, dividing into four teams may be a problem for your group. Instead, let individuals take on the group responsibilities as described in the session. But rather than creating pressure by having kids respond in turn, let everyone respond simultaneously. As Nathan makes his accusations against David, let all of your group members act out David's potential responses *at the same time*. David #1 will think of someone else to blame. David #2 will come up with all of the excuses he can think of. David #3 will have an easier time ignoring Nathan with all of the others present. And David #4 will begin to take responsibility. The different Davids should not acknowledge each other, but should respond to Nathan instead. Afterward, point out that the scene is not unlike a normal group of junior highers (or even adults) when someone begins making accusations. In any group of people, the four distinct responses are likely to arise.

Step 1

Rather than using Repro Resource 8, begin the session with a game of "Who Did It?" You will call out a list of famous achievements. When you call out an achievement, group members must tell you who did it. For instance, if you were to call out **Most career home runs in the history of major league baseball,** kids should answer "Hank Aaron." The first person to call out the correct answer gets a point. The person with the most points at the end of the game is the winner. To add some fun to the game, you might call out achievements that are unique to your group. For instance, you might call out **First person to capsize his canoe at last year's retreat** or **Won this year's pie-eating contest.** Use this activity to introduce the idea of taking responsibility for one's actions.

Step 4

Have kids form teams. Assign each team one of the situations on Repro Resource 9. Instruct each team to come up with a roleplay that illustrates a response to its assigned situation—as well as the consequences of that response. Give the teams a few minutes to work. When everyone's finished, have each team perform its roleplay. Discuss as a group which responses involve taking responsibility for one's actions. If you have time, you might ask each team to come up with a second roleplay—one that illustrates a response to the follow-up scenario.

Step 2

If your kids will find the situations in Step 2 to be clichéd, try the following ones instead. (1) **Caitlin and her boyfriend, ninth graders who call themselves Christians, have been sexually involved for two months. At first Caitlin felt guilty, but no more. Now she's mostly nervous about getting pregnant. She's decided to "take responsibility" by getting birth control pills from the school-based clinic. Mouse or woman?** (2) **Alan's parents just told him that they're getting a divorce. He's decided to "take responsibility" by trying to get them back together. Mouse or man?** (3) **Ron, fifteen, has feelings that lead him to think he's gay. He's decided to "take responsibility" for his own life by "coming out of the closet." Mouse or man?** Point out that these cases aren't simple. Caitlin may be taking responsibility for avoiding pregnancy, but she's not taking responsibility for obeying God. Alan is trying to take responsibility for someone *else's* actions—which is impossible and will leave him feeling like a failure. Ron is trying to take responsibility for something he can't be sure of; he needs counseling to help him sort out his feelings, and to help him see that God wants to give him a life that's full—without homosexual activity.

Step 4

Kids may be tired of lectures on growing up and taking responsibility (and may connect such lectures with commands to take out garbage and feed pets). Take a few minutes to brainstorm some of the *appealing* responsibilities that may await kids: driving, choosing movies and videos, dating, deciding when to go to sleep and when to wake up, picking a church, etc. Note that making solid choices in situations like those on Repro Resource 9 is good practice for handling the responsibilities that kids look forward to.

Step 3

David's sins in connection to his relationship with Bathsheba are familiar to most church people. However, for kids who are just beginning to read the Bible, II Samuel 11:2-17 is a significant passage. Your kids probably know about David and Goliath. They probably know that David was a great king. But that David could be guilty of sins like adultery and murder might be news to your kids. Give kids plenty of time to soak in what you're reading and ask questions. Only after they realize the gravity of David's sins will they be able to appreciate the fact that he accepted responsibility for his sinful behavior. Ask: **When we sin, how do you think our lives would be different if we immediately confessed what we did wrong rather than lying about it, trying to cover it up, or otherwise denying it?**

Step 4

As you wrap up the session, read Galatians 6:1-5. Ask kids to paraphrase what Paul is saying. Then ask: **Why are we told to carry each other's burdens in verse 2, but to carry our own load in verse 5?** Explain that no one is supposed to "coast" through his or her Christian life. We're supposed to do our share. Yet sometimes we face very strong trials that weigh us down. When we see someone in that condition, it's our responsibility to do what we can to help bear the person's burden. Our turn will come soon enough. Have group members write down one thing they can do during the coming week to take more responsibility for their own Christian life. Then have them write down a specific situation in which they can help "carry the burden" of someone else. Have kids report back next week to see if they actually did what they said they would do.

Step 1

To begin the session, have kids lie on the floor shoulder to shoulder, forming two straight lines. (Kids need to be squeezed tightly together in order for this activity to work.) Explain that the first person at the end of each line will be "passed" down the line by the others. The person being passed must remain very stiff and proceed head first, face up, down the line. When the first person being passed reaches the end, he or she lies down next to the last person and becomes a "passer." The next person at the beginning of the line is then passed down in the same manner. The first team to pass everyone along is the winner. Afterward, ask: **How did it feel to get passed along?** (Probably not very good, especially if one was dropped!) Point out that the same thing is true about responsibility—people often pass it along to the next person, and that's when things get dropped.

Step 4

Ask your kids to think about what the world—and their lives—would be like if God weren't a responsible God. Challenge them to think about how different the world would be; then have them create a mural depicting some of their ideas. Read I Corinthians 14:33. Then spend a few minutes in prayer, thanking God that He is a God of order and responsibility. Ask Him to help your group members as they begin to accept responsibility for their actions.

Step 3

To help your girls consider what it's like to be on the other side when someone won't take responsibility for his or her actions, have them put themselves in Bathsheba's place. King David has called her to him, slept with her, gotten her pregnant, tried to make it look like her husband's the father, and then had him killed. Ask them to think about the following questions, and then write their responses as though they're Bathsheba writing in a journal. **How do you feel about King David? What would you like to say to him?** When they've finished writing, talk about the fact that what we do—and how we respond to what we do—can have profound effects on other people's lives.

Step 4

Ask for volunteers to roleplay the scenarios in Repro Resource 9. You can act out each situation several times, getting different responses and corresponding conse- quences. Afterward, ask: **Why is it sometimes difficult not only to take responsibility for our actions, but also to choose to do the right thing in the first place? What can we do to help us make wise decisions and become more responsible?**

Step 2

After you read through the "Man or Mouse" choices, challenge each group member to come up with one example of a time when he was a "Man" and a second example of a time when he was a "Mouse." Let guys share their "Mouse" stories first. (It will probably help everyone feel more at ease if you begin with a story of your own.) Don't let anyone "mouse" out of this part of the exercise. Follow these stories with instances in which guys were "men," and felt good about the decisions they made and the responsibility they took during a difficult time. Challenge your guys to keep both stories in mind in the future. They can learn from their shortcomings as well as their successes.

Step 3

After the Bible study, ask: **Do you relate more to David or to Nathan? Why?** After your guys respond, point out that David is a dynamic person to relate to, even with all of his failures. He always seemed to be doing something exciting. He was a natural leader. On the other hand, we have Nathan. He too was a dynamic individual—when he needed to be. Have your guys consider what it must have been like to confront the very popular king of God's people and tell him that you knew he had been fooling around. Nathan remained tuned in to God's leading, even when David was drifting away. Suggest that many guys want to be "kings" (leaders), but not many dream of being prophets who stay in the background and serve God. Certainly, God uses Davids and Nathans, but very few of us can be leaders. Many more of us will be called to serve God in small and seemingly insignificant ways. While dreaming of being the guy on top, we must not forget to be guys who serve. When David forgot that, he got into serious trouble.

Step 1

Play a quick game of Simon Says to begin your session. Make it a difficult round, doing whatever it takes to trip people up. (For instance, change your tone of voice and say, **You guys pull closer together to get out of the doorway.** But if they move without your saying "Simon Says," they're out!) As people are eliminated, listen for complaints and excuses. Don't do anything at this time, but later in the session you can refer to such comments as you discuss the reluctance of some people to take responsibility for their own actions.

Step 4

At the end of the session, serve some kind of dessert such as cake or cookies. On the dessert should be written the word "Responsibility" in frosting or some other delectable topping. After closing in prayer and asking God for courage for your group members to take responsibility for their actions, point out that sometimes (as in this case) taking "responsibility" isn't nearly as difficult or unpleasant as it might sound.

Step 1

Plant a hidden video camera in your meeting place—perhaps behind a pile of books, with only the lens uncovered. Switch on the camera and leave the room. Delay your arrival at the meeting; pre-arrange with a volunteer to instigate a prank in your absence (drawing unflattering cartoons of you on the board, putting honey on your chair, etc.). Make sure that the camera is positioned so that it will catch the prank. (Your volunteer should try discreetly to keep other kids from blocking the camera's view too.) When you enter and "discover" the prank, demand to know who's behind it. When no one confesses, reveal your hidden camera and play the tape back. Use this activity to introduce the idea of taking responsibility for one's actions.

Step 4

Show a clip of one of the following videos (after prescreening it first) to illustrate how failing to take responsibility can lead to big problems. Ask: **How did this person try to avoid taking responsibility? What happened as a result? How do you think this person might have handled the situations on Repro Resource 9 when he or she was in junior high?**

• *All the President's Men.* Show a scene in which President Nixon denies having a role in the Watergate cover-up. Then show the scene in which Nixon has to resign.

• *Parenthood.* Play a scene in which Larry (Tom Hulce) refuses to take responsibility for his child or his gambling addiction, causing trouble for his father (Jason Robards).

• *Three Men and a Baby.* Show a scene in which Jack (Ted Danson) tries to avoid responsibility for the baby he's fathered, then has a hard time taking care of her.

Step 1

Try a shorter opener. Before the session, fill three clear quart jars with water. Add eight drops of red food coloring to one jar, eight drops of blue to another, and eight drops of green to the third. Stir the water and seal the jars. Then fill three more identical jars with water (no coloring) and seal them. Bring all of the jars and the bottles of food coloring to your meeting. Have kids form three teams. Instruct each team to choose a representative. Give each team one of the colored-water jars, the corresponding bottle of food coloring, and a clear-water jar. Each representative must decide in thirty seconds how many drops of coloring to put in his or her team's jar to match the color intensity of the premixed jar. The decision may be made after consulting with other team members, but must be made *before* putting the drops in the water. The team that comes up with the closest match gets a prize. Afterward, ask the representatives how it felt to make the final decision alone. Use this activity to introduce the issue of taking responsibility. In Step 2, skip the cases of Tyrone and Jennifer.

Step 3

Instead of having kids create and perform roleplays about what David might have said, simply say to the group: **Let's say that David blames someone else for what he did. What do you think he might tell Nathan? Or maybe he makes an excuse for what he did. In that case, what might he tell Nathan?** After hearing responses, move to the last paragraph of Step 3 in the session plan. In Step 4, use only one of the situations on Repro Resource 9.

Step 3

Ask your group members to share some examples (without using any names) of situations they know of in which someone didn't take responsibility for his or her actions. Ask: **What happened as a result? What might have happened if the person had taken responsibility for his or her actions?** If possible, be prepared with an example of your own.

Step 4

Replace Situation 1 on Repro Resource 9 with the following:

• While you're hanging out with a group of friends, someone dares you to throw a rock from an overpass at the cars below. Not wanting to look like a wimp in front of your friends, you take the dare. You throw the rock, hoping to miss any cars. No such luck. As your friends run away, you hear the sound of screeching tires and breaking glass. What do you do? What might some of the consequences of that choice be? *Follow-up*—The next Sunday in church, you overhear your pastor talking about someone in the church who was injured by a rock thrown from an overpass. The pastor asks you if you know anything about the incident. What do you do? What might some of the consequences of that choice be?

Step 2

Ask for volunteers from among your high schoolers to talk about times when they've been in situations similar to those listed in Step 2 and how they reacted. If they accepted the responsibility, what happened? If they didn't accept the responsibility, what happened? Encourage your junior highers to ask questions (though you may need to control the questioning so that it doesn't turn into prying). If none of your high schoolers are willing, be prepared to share some examples of your own.

Step 4

Make the following changes to Repro Resource 9:
• *Situation 1*—Your English teacher has assigned the following topic for your next term paper: "The Bible—Mythology at Its Best." You don't feel right about agreeing that the Bible is just a myth. What do you do? What might be some of the consequences of that choice? *Follow-up*—You write the paper, agreeing that the Bible is great literature, but arguing that it is truth—and not a myth. Your paper comes back with an "F" on it and a note saying, "This was a well-written paper, but not the right topic." What do you do? What might be some of the consequences of that choice?

Step 1

Rather than using Repro Resource 8, begin the session with a variation of the game "Seven Up." Ask for three or more (depending on the size of your group) volunteers to come to the front of the room. Have the rest of your group members close their eyes. (You might also ask them to cover their eyes with their hands to make sure that none of them peeks.) Instruct each of your volunteers to wander around the room and tag one person on top of the head. Then have the volunteers regather at the front of your room. Instruct the rest of the kids to open their eyes. Those who were tagged must try to guess which of the volunteers tagged them. If a person guesses correctly, he or she takes the volunteer's place at the front of the room. If not, the original volunteer remains. Play as many rounds as you have time for. Afterward, use the "Who did it?" angle of the game to introduce the idea of taking responsibility for one's actions.

Step 2

After you go through the scenarios in Step 2, ask: **Have you ever taken responsibility for an action, even though you knew that you'd probably get in trouble for it? If so, why did you do it? How did you feel after you took responsibility for the action? What might have happened if you hadn't taken responsibility for the action?** Encourage several kids to respond. If possible, be prepared to share an example of your own. Then move on to Step 3.

Date Used:

Approx. Time

Step 1: It's Your Choice _____
o Small Group
o Large Group
o Fellowship & Worship
o Extra Fun
o Media
o Short Meeting Time
o Sixth Grade
Things needed:

Step 2: The Mouse Test _____
o Heard It All Before
o Mostly Guys
o Combined Junior High/High School
o Sixth Grade
Things needed:

Step 3: Response-o-rama _____
o Extra Action
o Small Group
o Little Bible Background
o Mostly Girls
o Mostly Guys
o Short Meeting Time
o Urban
Things needed:

Step 4: Face the Consequences _____
o Extra Action
o Large Group
o Heard It All Before
o Little Bible Background
o Fellowship & Worship
o Mostly Girls
o Extra Fun
o Media
o Urban
o Combined Junior High/High School
Things needed:

YOUR GOALS FOR THIS SESSION:

Choose one or more

☐ To help kids recognize the temporal nature of the world's definition of success.

☐ To help kids understand the difference between the world's definition of success and God's definition of success.

☐ To help kids choose one action that will move them toward success according to God's definition.

☐ Other _____

Your Bible Base:

Joshua 1:1-9
Mark 9:33-37

STEP
I

Burst Out

(Needed: Prizes)

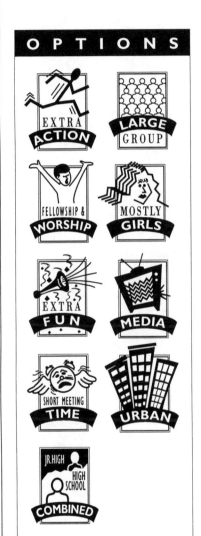

OPTIONS

Have kids form two teams. Explain that one at a time, you will give each team a category. After you've read the category, the team will have one minute to call out as many items in that category as possible. The team will get one point for each item it comes up with that matches one of the answers on the following master list. If possible, enlist an assistant (perhaps an adult volunteer) to help you listen for answers. This activity can get pretty hectic!

After you announce the first category, give Team 1 one minute to shout out answers. Keep track of how many items on the master list the team names. When time is up, announce the team's score, identifying which items on the master list were named and which were missed. Then announce the second category for Team 2 and continue the process. (There are four categories, so each team will be able to play two rounds.) The team with the most points at the end of the game is the winner. Award prizes (perhaps bite-size candy bars) to members of the winning team.

The categories and master lists for the game are as follows:

Category #1: Signs of Success
  1. Big house
  2. Money/wealth
  3. Expensive clothes
  4. Good job
  5. Influence
  6. Power
  7. Investments
  8. Fame
  9. Nice car
  10. Exotic vacations

Category #2: Successful Actors and Actresses
[NOTE: This list was compiled in 1994. You may need to modify it to accommodate current popular actors and actresses or to eliminate people who are no longer popular.]
  1. Mel Gibson
  2. Tom Hanks
  3. Julia Roberts
  4. Harrison Ford
  5. Sylvester Stallone
  6. Arnold Schwarzenegger
  7. Kevin Costner
  8. Alec Baldwin
  9. Meg Ryan
10. Jodie Foster

Category #3: Successful People in History
  1. Winston Churchill
  2. Henry Ford
  3. Albert Einstein
  4. Babe Ruth
  5. Abraham Lincoln
  6. Thomas Edison
  7. Charles Lindbergh
  8. John F. Kennedy
  9. Benjamin Franklin
10. George Washington

Category #4: Successful Professions
  1. Businessperson
  2. Lawyer
  3. Actor/actress
  4. Professor
  5. Politician
  6. Doctor
  7. Rock musician
  8. Banker
  9. Professional athlete
10. Judge

Use this activity to lead in to a discussion on what success is.

Success Is . . .

(Needed: Bibles, copies of Repro Resource 10, copies of Repro Resource 11, pencils)

Hand out copies of "Success Rebus"(Repro Resource 10) and pencils. Let kids work in pairs or small groups to solve the rebus puzzles on the right side of the sheet and then match them with the correct names on the left side of the sheet.

Give group members a few minutes to work. When everyone is finished, go through the sheet as a group, asking kids to shout out their responses. The correct answers are as follows: Howard Hughes—making tons of money; the Wright Brothers—being the first to fly; Michelangelo—painting ceilings of churches; Joshua—knowing and doing what God said.

Afterward, ask: **How many of you were surprised to find Joshua's name included on a list of successful people? After all, as far as we know, Joshua wasn't a wealthy man and he didn't invent anything.** Get a few comments from your group members regarding Joshua's success.

Say: **Before we get too far into our discussion, maybe we'd better decide what success is. After all, not everyone agrees on what it means to be successful. Let's take a quick look at the difference between the world's definition of success and God's definition of success.**

Hand out copies of "What's Success?" (Repro Resource 11). Ideally, your group members should still have their pencils from filling out Repro Resource 10.

Ask: **If you could narrow down the world's definition of success to three words, what words would you choose?** Entertain any answers that group members come up with.

Then refer kids to the three rebuses in the "World's Definition" section of Repro Resource 11. The rebuses are pretty simple. Have kids shout out the answers as soon as they figure them out. The correct answers are "money," "power," and "fame." Have group members write these three words next to the appropriate rebuses on the sheet.

Ask: **Why do you think our culture has decided that these are the things that make someone successful?** (Perhaps because these things appear to give people the freedom or ability to do whatever they want.)

Is there anything wrong with having these three things?
(Not necessarily—it depends on how you use them.)

Say: **Let's take a look at what Jesus said to some guys who were searching for this kind of success.**

Have group members turn in their Bibles to Mark 9:33-37. Ask someone to read the passage aloud. Then ask: **What were the disciples arguing about?** (They were arguing about which of them was the greatest.)

How did Jesus respond to them? (He said that whoever wants to be first must be last, the servant of all.)

Say: **It seems from Jesus' response that God's definition of success must be very different from the world's definition. But that doesn't mean God defines success as being poor, wimpy, and unknown. Let's look at the example of Joshua.**

Ask group members to turn in their Bibles to Joshua 1:1-9. Have someone read the passage aloud. Emphasize that the end of verse 8 says that Joshua will be successful if he follows the Lord's commands.

Refer group members to the "God's Definition" section of Repro Resource 11. Explain that the Lord's definition of success is "knowing and doing what God says." Three examples of this can be found in Joshua 1:6-8. Give group members a few minutes to read the passage and then fill in the blanks on Repro Resource 11. When everyone is finished, ask volunteers to share their responses. The correct answers are as follows:

- Be strong and courageous (1:6, 7)
- Obey God (1:7b)
- Read and study the Bible (1:8)

STEP 3

Compare and Contrast

Use the following questions to help your group members better understand the differences between the world's definition of success and God's definition. During this discussion time, keep in mind that the successes of the world are pummeled into kids' brains daily by every aspect of their culture. And to be honest, God's definition of success can look fairly dull to a culturally brainwashed junior higher.

Ask: **What do you have to do to maintain success in the**

O P T I O N S

world's eyes once you get it? (Be lucky; be careful to do exactly the right things.)

How easy is it to lose success in the world's eyes? Explain.

What do you have to do to maintain success in God's eyes once you get it? (Continue doing the things that gave you success in the first place.)

How easy is it to lose success in God's eyes? Explain.

Which definition of success will bring you more real happiness? Encourage kids to respond honestly here. They may have a hard time with this. They'll know they should say "God's," but might not really think so.

If you have success in the world's eyes, what do you have to worry about? (Losing your money or fame or having it taken from you; people who have more power than you do; people deciding that you're not famous anymore.)

If you have success in God's eyes, what do you have to worry about? (Nothing.)

Why might God's definition of success not always sound as good as the world's definition?

How long does success in the world's eyes last? (Anywhere from a moment to most of a lifetime.)

How long does success in God's eyes last? (Forever.)

STEP 4

My Step toward Success

(Needed: Index cards, pencils, chalkboard and chalk or newsprint and marker)

O P T I O N S

Instruct your group members to brainstorm a list of things they can do to move toward God's definition of success. Write their ideas on the board. These ideas might include reading the Bible regularly, learning what some of the hard-to-understand passages of the Bible mean, standing up for God at school, and obeying parents.

After you've gotten several ideas listed, hand out an index card to each person. The kids should still have pencils, though the writing utensils may have disintegrated into small shards of wood and graphite by now!

Ask your group members to choose one idea from the list on the board or to come up with an idea of their own. Then have them write on the index card "My step toward success is . . . ," filling in the idea on their cards.

As you wrap up the session, allow for a few minutes of silent prayer, during which time group members can ask God for courage and discipline to follow through with their idea. When the prayer time is over, suggest to your kids that they put their card on their dresser, in the corner of their bedroom mirror, or somewhere else where they'll see it regularly.

SUCCESS REBUS

*Solve the word puzzles on the right; then match
them with the correct person on the left.*

THIS PERSON . . .   BECAME SUCCESSFUL BY . . .

Howard
Hughes

 SEAL + RINGS– R; DOVE – D;

The Wright
Brothers

 +  ;  ; OF;

Michaelangelo   NO + –K; AND; + ; ;  –L.

Joshua

 + –R; THE;  ; 2;

W H A T ' S
S·U·C·C·E·S·S ?

WORLD'S DEFINITION

1.

2.  **+ R**

3. **— L**

GOD'S DEFINITION

1. __ __ __ __ __ __ __   __ __ __   __ __ __ __ __ __ __ __ __

2. __ __ __ __   __ __ __

3. __ __ __ __   __ __ __   __ __ __ __ __   __ __ __   __ __ __ __ __

Step 1

Bring in a package of plastic shower curtain rings. Dump the rings in the middle of the floor. Have kids take off their shoes and sit in a circle around the pile of rings. Say: **Have you ever heard the expression "going for the brass ring"?** Explain that the expression refers to putting everything you've got into a chance to be successful. Then say: **Here are the brass rings. Your goal is to get as many rings on your toes as you can in thirty seconds—using only your feet. The person wearing the most rings in thirty seconds wins. No kicking. Go!** After the contest, discuss what kids' real "brass rings"—their symbols of success—are.

Step 3

Have kids form two teams. Explain that Team A members will try to push each other aside to get a bag of cookies in the middle of the room. The winner keeps all of the cookies. Members of Team B, using another bag, will then serve one cookie to each "loser" from Team A. Finally, reward each person from Team B with two cookies from a third bag. Ask: **Which team got the better deal? Why? Which suffered more stress? How is Team A like those following the world's idea of success? How is Team B like those following God's idea?** In Step 4, let each person choose either a "valuable" Styrofoam ball (which you've painted gold) or a "lowly" Ping-Pong ball (which you've smudged with dirt). Then let kids throw the balls against an outside wall to see which kind bounces better. Use this as a reminder that when we reach for God's idea of success, we bounce back from failures more easily than when we strive for fame and fortune.

Step 2

After you discuss Joshua and his success, ask: **What do you think made Joshua a success to begin with?** Perhaps someone will be familiar with Joshua's personal history as one of the spies who were sent by Moses into the promised land to check things out. When the twelve spies reported, only Joshua and Caleb advised the people to move ahead. They had faith that God would continue to take care of the people as He always had. But Joshua and Caleb were outnumbered, outvoted, and almost put to death by their own people (Numbers 13:26–14:10). Point out that it took the faith of a small group—a *very* small group of two people—to get to the point where the session picks up with Joshua's life. Encourage members of your own small group to remain faithful even though their numbers are somewhat low. Like Joshua, they will eventually be rewarded if their faith remains strong.

Step 3

Rather than having kids respond as individuals to the questions about success in this step, ask the questions in terms of your entire small group. Discuss God's success and worldly success in terms of your group. The world is looking for big numbers and big budgets to determine success. But is that what God is looking for? Discussing the group as a whole is a lot less threatening than asking junior highers to examine themselves. But after you deal with the entire group, kids should be better able to shift the discussion to a personal level.

Step 1

Begin the session with a team spelling contest. Have kids form two teams. Explain that one at a time, you will give each team a word to spell. But rather than spelling the word out loud, team members must form the letters of the word with their bodies by lying on the floor in various positions. Every team member must be involved in the spelling of the word. Award a point for each word that is spelled correctly and recognizably (you be the judge). The team with the most points at the end of the game is the winner. Make sure that the last word you use for the spelling contest is "success." After the contest, go through Step 1 as written.

Step 2

Rather than having kids fill out Repro Resource 10, give them an opportunity to create their own "success rebuses." Draw the rebuses from Repro Resource 10 on the board to give your kids an idea of what you're looking for. Then let volunteers come to the board one at a time to draw their own rebuses that describe how famous people became successful. See how long it takes the rest of the group to decipher each rebus and figure out who's being described. After several volunteers have had an opportunity to draw, move on to the Repro Resource 11 activity.

O P T I O N S

S E S S I O N F I V E

Step 2

Kids may yawn at the revelation that they should be strong and courageous, obey God, and study the Bible. If so, write these actions, along with "be a servant," on the left side of the board. Then brainstorm a list of things a person must do to be successful in the world's eyes (get rich, become a great athlete, be born with good looks, practice a skill for hours every day, beat everyone competing against you, etc.); write these things on the right side of the board. Ask: **How many people in this group can do the things on the right side?** (Few, if any.) **How many can do the things on the left side?** (Everyone can, to the best of his or her ability.) Point out that under God's definition, everyone can be a success. If the definition sounds boring, maybe that's because God's idea of success is within our reach—if we belong to Him and rely on His power.

Step 3

When the alternatives are fortune and fame, how can you get kids to consider a life of servanthood and obedience? Try asking kids how many of these former top-of-the-charts performers are still big today: Milli Vanilli, The Bee Gees, George Michael, Boy George, Irene Cara, Herb Alpert, Lulu, The Archies, and New Kids on the Block. Ask: **What happens to celebrities as they get older?** (Many fade into obscurity, even poverty.) Bring in one to three older people from your church who are still vital and happy about serving God. Interview these people about whether they feel their lives have been worthwhile so far. What are their definitions of success? Would they trade their experiences as Christians for a few years of fame? Do they wish they'd spent more time making money? What are their goals for the future?

Step 2

Focus on the varying opinions regarding success in this step; back up what you're saying with the Joshua 1:1-9 passage. Save the Mark 9:33-37 passage for the next step. After group members give their definitions of success, have them individually read Joshua 1:1-9. Ask: **Based on what God is telling Joshua in this passage, would you consider yourself to be a success? What would you need to do in order to become more "success-ful"? What promises does God make to Joshua? What does God expect from Joshua in return?** If your group members don't know this story, don't rush through it. Help them learn to read and absorb important spiritual truths on their own.

Step 3

If you postponed the Mark 9:33-37 passage from Step 2 (see the "Little Bible Background" option for Step 2), use it here. Some of your kids may be surprised to discover that Jesus' own disciples got into arguments about who was number one. Ask: **Have you ever been in an argument in which you tried to prove that you were better than someone else? If so, were you successful? What are some ways we can serve the other people in this group rather than trying to demand our own way? What do you think Jesus saw in little children that caused Him to use one as a model for how we should behave?**

Step 1

Have kids form teams. Give each team a piece of newsprint large enough for members to draw a life-sized body. Explain that you're going to have a contest to find the most successful person in the world, whom the teams are going to create. Provide the members of each team with creative supplies and have them prepare their "person" for success. After a few minutes, have each team describe its individual and what it is about the person that makes him or her successful. Afterward, ask: **What is success?** Get several responses. **What do you think God's definition of success is?**

Step 4

Have kids reassemble into the teams they formed for the "most successful person in the world" contest (see the "Fellowship & Worship" option for Step 1). Provide teams with creative supplies again. This time, instruct the members of each team to portray what they think God would consider to be a success. Encourage them to think creatively; they might portray anything from a sunset that God created to a person helping someone in need. You may wish to read Matthew 6:25-33 as food for thought while they work. After a few minutes, review the new collages; then thank God for His perspective on success.

Step 1

Substitute the following categories for your opening activity:

• *Category #2: Successful Actresses*—
(1) Julia Roberts; (2) Meg Ryan; (3) Meryl Streep; (4) Jodie Foster; (5) Susan Sarandon; (6) Sharon Stone; (7) Winona Ryder; (8) Glenn Close; (9) Melanie Griffith; (10) Juliette Lewis

• *Category #3: Successful Women in History*—(1) Joan of Arc; (2) Florence Nightingale; (3) Marie Curie; (4) Mother Teresa; (5) Margaret Thatcher; (6) Emily Dickinson; (7) Susan B. Anthony; (8) Cleopatra; (9) Queen Esther; (10) Babe Didrikson Zaharias

Step 3

Have kids form groups of three or four. Give each group paper and pencils. Instruct each group to list the names of women in the Bible who were successful and explain why each woman was a success. Challenge the groups to list as many women as possible. After a few minutes, have each group share its list. Then say: **There's nothing in the Bible that says you must be a man to be a success!** Encourage your girls to live lives that are successful for the Lord.

Step 2

Rather than having your guys fill out Repro Resource 10, ask them to spend the next few minutes acting "successful." Whatever they think the word entails, they should do what they can to act it out. Watch them to see if some try to boss others around, begin to swagger across the room, or do anything else that reflects a shallow, worldly concept of success. After a few minutes, announce that you want to reward the ones who did the best job of acting out "success." Give prizes to those who didn't automatically become obnoxious and offensive to those around them. Then move on to Repro Resource 11.

Step 4

Most guys are competitive by nature. But they've already seen from Mark 9:33-37 that competing to be number one is not something that pleases God. If you think your guys can handle the competition without missing the point, challenge them to conduct a servanthood contest during the following week. As they brainstorm ways to be more "successful" from God's perspective, see if you can foster a little good-natured rivalry among your guys. If John sets a goal to be "twice the servant" that Bill is, and Bill takes the challenge, spiritual growth can be fun for guys. You do need to be careful, however, that all glory from the competition goes to God. You want your guys to grow in grace, and not develop a false sense of pride for their efforts.

Step 1

Since you opened the session with a homemade version of the game Outburst, be aware that "Bible Outburst" also exists (a trademark of Hersch & Company, © 1989, produced in the U.S.A. by Western Publishing Company). If your group members enjoy this kind of competition, find the game and let them play before or after the session. It's also an excellent resource to pull out from time to time when you need to fill periods of time and haven't prepared anything. And if you pay attention while kids are playing, you may be able to determine what areas of Scripture kids may be weak in, allowing you to prepare more effective sessions in the future.

Step 4

As a conclusion or follow-up to this session, show a video that portrays the life of a truly successful person such as Corrie ten Boom *(The Hiding Place)* or Eric Liddel *(Chariots of Fire)*. It's one thing to talk about being successful for God by serving others, but seeing what it can accomplish can have a much stronger effect on junior highers.

Step 1

During the week before the session, use your VCR to record the closing credits—just the credits—of several shows. Include some "rolling" credits from TV movies. Record a total of about one minute of credits. Before playing them back for the group, hand out paper and pencils. Say: **Many people would say that working in Hollywood makes you a success. I'm going to show you the names of some of these successful people. As you watch, write down the ones you think are the biggest successes.** After showing the tape, have kids share what they wrote. Ask: **How did you decide who the biggest successes were? If your name was in these credits, would you feel like a success? Why or why not? Would it make a difference if your name was bigger than other names, or on the screen longer? What do you think makes a person a success?**

Step 3

Play and discuss one or more contemporary Christian songs that contrast the world's view of success with God's view. Possibilities include "Meltdown (At Madame Tussaud's)" (Steve Taylor), "People in a Box" (Farrell and Farrell), "Gotta Have the Real Thing" (Rick Riso), "Not of This World" (Petra), "Ordinary People" (Danniebelle Hall), "Losing Game" (Dallas Holm and Praise), and "God's Own Fool" (Michael Card).

Step 1

Try a shorter opener. Bring five paper plates that you've numbered (on the bottom, out of sight) from one to five. Bring a large bag of candies, too. Place the plates randomly on the floor. Let each person find a unique object (a coin, sock, etc.) to represent himself or herself. Explain that each plate is numbered on the bottom, and that the number stands for the number of candies that will be won for tossing an item onto that plate. Standing back from the plates, kids should decide which one to toss their items onto. After items are thrown, have kids form two teams. *Then* look under the plates to see how many candies each person won. Award the candies. Then give *extra* candy to the team whose members already won more candy. Ask: **Was this a game of skill or chance? Who was a success in this game? Is being successful in life a matter of skill or chance? Why? How can you tell who's a success in life?**

Step 4

In place of Step 4, brainstorm three mistakes that a kid could make at school (tripping in the lunch line, studying the wrong chapter for a test, etc.). Ask: **If you're aiming for the world's idea of success, how could mistakes like these really mess you up?** (Clumsiness could put you on the "geek" list; a bad grade might hurt your chances of getting into college and making lots of money later; etc.) **If you're aiming for God's idea of success, would mistakes like these be so serious?** (No, because we could still grow in our ability to obey Him and serve others.) Close by encouraging kids with the thought that aiming for God's idea of success can make it easier to bounce back from goofs and failures.

Step 1

Rather than using the "Burst Out" game, begin the session with an activity called "What Is Success?" Explain that you will read a list of items one at a time. If group members think that an item indicates success, they should stand; if they don't think that an item necessarily represents success, they should remain seated. Among the items you might name are "having an article written about you in the newspaper," "getting a standing ovation in front of a large crowd of people," "getting a job," "becoming a parent," "being loved by someone of the opposite sex," "owning a large house," "being able to do whatever you want whenever you want," and "winning the lottery." (Feel free to add any other items that you can think of.) Afterward, ask: **How would you define success?** You'll want to refer to group members' responses later in the session when you talk about the difference between the world's definition of success and God's definition of success.

Step 2

Rather than using Repro Resource 10, try another option. Before the session, make "celebrity flash cards" by writing the names of various successful people on large index cards, one name per card. As you hold up the cards one at a time, ask kids to call out what each person is successful at. For instance, Michael Jordan is successful at basketball; Rosie Perez is successful at acting; Anita Baker is successful at singing; Nelson Mandela is successful at fighting apartheid. Make sure that the last flash card has "Joshua" written on it. See if your kids know what this Bible character was successful at. If no one mentions it, point out that he was successful at knowing and doing what God said. Then move on to the Repro Resource 11 activity.

Step 1

At the end of Step 1 (and in lieu of using Repro Resource 10 in Step 2), ask: **What do you think the world's definition of success is?** Get several responses; then write a condensed summary of your kids' definitions on the board. Ask: **Who are some people you can think of, living or dead, who fit this definition?** Get several responses. Then ask: **What do you think God's definition of success is?** Write a condensed summary of your kids' definitions on the board. Then brainstorm as a group some people who fit that definition. Spend a few minutes discussing the differences between the world's definition of success and God's definition. Also discuss how difficult (or easy) it was to name people who offer an example of God-honoring success.

Step 2

Skip Repro Resource 11. Ask: **If you could narrow the world's definition of success to three words, what words would you choose?** After you've gone through Mark 9:33-37, have someone read aloud Matthew 6:14-21. Point out that the verses from Matthew can be applied to the world's three symbols of success. Verses 14 and 15 refer to forgiving others. Often when we don't forgive, we do so because we think that will give us power over someone else. Verses 16-18 refer to fame. The hypocrites wanted to be noticed, wanted the spotlight, wanted recognition. And verses 19-21 are obviously about money and wealth. Based on Matthew 6:14-21 and Mark 9:33-37, have your kids come up with three words to summarize God's definition of success.

Step 2

Rather than using Repro Resource 10 with your sixth graders, try another activity. Before the session, you'll need to gather pictures of several famous and successful people throughout history. At this point in the session, hold up two of the pictures at a time. Ask: **Which of these people is more successful? Why?** Emphasize that you're not asking which person is more famous or which person is better liked; you're asking which person is more successful. It should be interesting to hear your kids' views as to what makes someone successful. Lead in to a discussion on the difference between the world's definition of success and God's definition of success.

Step 3

After you've gone through Step 3 as written, ask your kids a few more questions: **Have you ever been successful in the world's eyes? If so, at what? Have you ever been successful in God's eyes? If so, at what?** Group members' responses should let you know whether they understand the difference between the world's definition of success and God's definition.

Date Used:

Approx.
Time

Step 1: Burst Out _____
o Extra Action
o Large Group
o Fellowship & Worship
o Mostly Girls
o Extra Fun
o Media
o Short Meeting Time
o Urban
o Combined Junior High/High School
Things needed:

Step 2: Success Is . . . _____
o Small Group
o Large Group
o Heard It All Before
o Little Bible Background
o Mostly Guys
o Urban
o Combined Junior High/High School
o Sixth Grade
Things needed:

Step 3: Compare and Contrast _____
o Extra Action
o Small Group
o Heard It All Before
o Little Bible Background
o Mostly Girls
o Media
o Sixth Grade
Things needed:

Step 4: My Step toward Success _____
o Fellowship & Worship
o Mostly Guys
o Extra Fun
o Short Meeting Time
Things needed:

Custom Curriculum Critique

Please take a moment to fill out this evaluation form, rip it out, fold it, tape it, and send it back to us. This will help us continue to customize products for you. Thanks!

1. Overall, please give this *Custom Curriculum* course (*Bouncing Back*) a grade in terms of how well it worked for you. (A=excellent; B=above average; C=average; D=below average; F=failure) Circle one.

A   B   C   D   F

2. Now assign a grade to each part of this curriculum that you used.

a. Upfront article	A	B	C	D	F	Didn't use
b. Publicity/Clip art	A	B	C	D	F	Didn't use
c. Repro Resource Sheets	A	B	C	D	F	Didn't use
d. Session 1	A	B	C	D	F	Didn't use
e. Session 2	A	B	C	D	F	Didn't use
f. Session 3	A	B	C	D	F	Didn't use
g. Session 4	A	B	C	D	F	Didn't use
h. Session 5	A	B	C	D	F	Didn't use

3. How helpful were the options?
   - ❏ Very helpful
   - ❏ Somewhat helpful
   - ❏ Not too helpful
   - ❏ Not at all helpful

4. Rate the amount of options:
   - ❏ Too many
   - ❏ About the right amount
   - ❏ Too few

5. Tell us how often you used each type of option (4=Always; 3=Sometimes; 2=Seldom; 1=Never)

	4	3	2	1
Extra Action	❏	❏	❏	❏
Combined Jr. High/High School	❏	❏	❏	❏
Urban	❏	❏	❏	❏
Small Group	❏	❏	❏	❏
Large Group	❏	❏	❏	❏
Extra Fun	❏	❏	❏	❏
Heard It All Before	❏	❏	❏	❏
Little Bible Background	❏	❏	❏	❏
Short Meeting Time	❏	❏	❏	❏
Fellowship and Worship	❏	❏	❏	❏
Mostly Guys	❏	❏	❏	❏
Mostly Girls	❏	❏	❏	❏
Media	❏	❏	❏	❏
Extra Challenge (High School only)	❏	❏	❏	❏
Sixth Grade (Jr. High only)	❏	❏	❏	❏

6. What did you like best about this course?

7. What suggestions do you have for improving *Custom Curriculum*?

8. Other topics you'd like to see covered in this series:

9. Are you?
    ❑ Full time paid youthworker
    ❑ Part time paid youthworker
    ❑ Volunteer youthworker

10. When did you use *Custom Curriculum*?
    ❑ Sunday School   ❑ Small Group
    ❑ Youth Group   ❑ Retreat
    ❑ Other _____

11. What grades did you use it with? _____

12. How many kids used the curriculum in an average week? _____

13. What's the approximate attendance of your entire Sunday school program (Nursery through Adult)? _____

14. If you would like information on other *Custom Curriculum* courses, or other youth products from David C. Cook, please fill out the following:

    Name: _____
    Church Name: _____
    Address: _____
                   _____

    Phone: (____) _____

                   Thank you!